COMMUNIC   NNECTS

To my grandson, Jackson Peter.
May he fulfil the potential God has placed in his life.

Communication that Connects

DAVID BEER

KINGSWAY PUBLICATIONS
EASTBOURNE

ISBN 0 85476 989 7

Published by
KINGSWAY COMMUNICATIONS LTD
Lottbridge Drive, Eastbourne, BN23 6NT, England.
Email: books@kingsway.co.uk

Designed and produced for the publishers by
Bookprint Creative Services, P.O. Box 827, BN21 3YJ, England.
Printed in Great Britain.

Contents

Preface

The first time I led worship on nationwide live television, I realized two things. First, I could not afford to waste any words. If we were going to make this a worthwhile worship experience for the hundreds of thousands of viewers who were joining us, then making the best use of the time available was a priority. Every sentence needed to count. Second, I knew that people had the choice of switching off. They had no obligation to sit through our 55-minute 40-second worship service, as did the congregation in the church. These two factors certainly focused my mind.

It is a strange experience at the beginning of a televised service. During the last 60 seconds before going on air, an ominous silence settles over the congregation. The floor manager stands at the back of the church with a raised hand. The moment he lowers it, we are on air. However, after the floor manager has lowered his hand, nothing appears to have changed. Everything seems the same as it was before. Yet everything has changed. We have been joined by an unseen congregation of up to a million people.

On these occasions I often think of the following verse:

> Therefore, since we are surrounded by such a great cloud of witnesses, let us throw off everything that hinders and the sin that so easily entangles, and let us run with perseverance the race marked out for us. (Hebrews 12:1)

I am very grateful for all that I have learned through my involvement with television over more than a decade. I am grateful to those who have trusted me to be in front of the camera, whether leading a worship service, preaching, taking part in discussion, being interviewed or introducing and presenting worship from churches of different denominations around the country. I am glad to have been included in programme planning and in researching churches and individuals to take part in religious programmes on the independent television network in the UK.

I am grateful to all the colleagues I have worked with over the years for the experience I have gained in so many areas. In particular, I would like to mention those on the production team for *Morning Worship* and later the *Sunday Morning* programme on ITV produced by Anglia TV: Eddie Anderson, Malcolm Allsop, Mike Talbot, Ann Rudland and Felicity Maton.

The disciplines of communicating on television in a way that connects with the viewers has taught me much as a local Christian minister. I wish every minister could have such tuition.

I still have a long way to go, however. I am continually learning. I am learning from my son-in-law, Steve Rouse, Pastor of Balham Baptist Church, South London; Also from my two present colleagues in ministry, Ben Marlowe, our Associate Pastor, and Phil Brown, our Youth Pastor. I am grateful for many mentors, including Lewis Drummond, holder of the Billy Graham Chair of Evangelism and Church Growth at Beeson Divinity School at Samford University, and Rick Warren, Senior Pastor of Saddleback Church, California.

Once again, my wife Dorothy has been very patient with me during the writing of this book. I am grateful for the encouragement of my family, my daughter Leisa and her husband Steve, my son Keith and his wife Faith. My grand-children always provide a challenge in their own way: Brianna, to whom my first book was dedicated, and Jackson, to whom this book is dedicated.

I would like to thank our church administrator, Jan Parmenter, for her secretarial skills and for copying and collating the pages of the manuscript.

Most of all I give credit to God, who has allowed me the privilege of being a small part of his strategy to communicate the good news of Jesus Christ in the twentieth and twenty-first centuries.

Introduction

One of the most exciting moments of my life was to stand in the entrance of the *Columbia* space shuttle as it sat on the launch pad at Kennedy Space Center just a few days prior to launch. An elevator had taken us up to the high level on the gantry where the astronauts cross the narrow steel walkway on to the shuttle. Looking in at the flight deck, I knew we were standing on top of an incredible source of raw power. Each of the two white rocket boosters on either side of the shuttle contained more than a million pounds of solid propellant. The shuttle's huge yellow external tank was loaded with more than 500,000 gallons of super-cold liquid oxygen and liquid hydrogen. When these are mixed and burned together they form the fuel for the shuttle's three main rocket engines. As a pilot, used to applying 'full power' for take-off in a light aircraft, I was awestruck at the thought of what full power would mean to the crew of *Columbia* as they flew a few days later.

The local Christian church stands on an even more incredible source of power. The apostle Paul wrote to the church in Corinth saying,

My message and my preaching were not with wise and persuasive words, but with a demonstration of the Spirit's power, so

11

that your faith might not rest on men's wisdom, but on God's power. (1 Corinthians 2:4–5)

Again, Paul says in Ephesians 1:18–20,

I pray also that the eyes of your heart may be enlightened in order that you may know the hope to which he has called you, the riches of his glorious inheritance in the saints, and his incomparably great power for us who believe. That power is like the working of his mighty strength, which he exerted in Christ when he raised him from the dead and seated him at his right hand in the heavenly realms.

When Paul is writing to Timothy he says, 'For God did not give us a spirit of timidity, but a spirit of power, of love and of self-discipline' (2 Timothy 1:7).

Finally, of course, we remember the words of Jesus to his disciples in Acts 1:8,

But you will receive power when the Holy Spirit comes on you; and you will be my witnesses in Jerusalem, and in all Judea and Samaria, and to the ends of the earth.

Most of the space shuttle's power is used up in the first few minutes of flight. It takes seven million pounds of thrust to lift the 68-ton vehicle off the launch pad. At launch, the shuttle's three main engines are fed with the liquid fuel from the big yellow tank. At first the shuttle rises slowly, but within 60 seconds it has accelerated to over 2,000 miles an hour. The yellow tank is discarded shortly before the shuttle reaches orbit. The two additional solid-fuel boosters are jettisoned after two minutes. The shuttle must reach speeds of about 17,500 miles per hour to remain in orbit.

In a similar way, getting the local church off the launch pad can take a great deal of power. One of the keys is effective communication. When the church was launched on the Day of Pentecost, Peter and the other disciples communicated powerfully and effectively. The twenty-first-century church needs to draw on the power of the Holy Spirit to communicate effectively today – but how do we do that?

Most individuals in the Western world receive an average of 30,000 messages each week. How can we break in to share the message of the gospel? Our responsibility is to convey the message of God's love and salvation to people in terms understandable to them, in their culture and circumstances, in their political situations, in their social realities, and in the light of whatever national events are shaping their lives and their thinking at that moment.

Where can we go to learn this important skill? Well, we already have the greatest textbook on communication – the Bible. We can learn from Jesus and the Gospels. We can learn from the book of Acts and the Epistles. We can observe the early evangelists in their actions and in their spoken and written communications.

The power needs to be connected to the word. Jesus told the Sadducees that they were in error because they did not know the Scriptures or the power of God (Matthew 22:29). What made the church so effective in its early life was what it *said* as well as what it *did*. That power showed itself to be effective against all the might of the Roman world.

We must not forget, however, that this is a power that appears weak in the eyes of the world.

> Brothers, think of what you were when you were called. Not many of you were wise by human standards; not many were influential; not many were of noble birth. But God chose the foolish things of the world to shame the wise; God chose the weak things of the world to shame the strong. (1 Corinthians 1:26–27)

Paul's experience of the power of God is expressed most clearly in his statement, 'For when I am weak, then I am strong' (2 Corinthians 12:10).

It is the power of God that gives life to our communication, but we also need wisdom. Proverbs 13:14 says, 'The teaching of the wise is a fountain of life, turning a man from the snares of death.' Proverbs 16:23–24 tell us, 'A wise man's heart guides his mouth, and his lips promote instruction. Pleasant words are a honeycomb, sweet to the soul and healing to the bones.'

Jesus spoke with power and authority, but also with wisdom. He is the master communicator from whom we can learn. He is 'the Word of God'.

PART 1

Yesterday, Today and For Ever

1

The Communication Revolution

The art of media communication has developed considerably over the years. If we were to compare a television weather forecast or news programme from 1965 with one from 1985, and then with one from today, we would notice big differences in language and style. Today the general style of such programmes is much more informal and conversational. Greater use is made of visual presentation and the graphics are, of course, hugely improved. The language is simpler and more direct. The purpose of the broadcasters is to report accurately, but also compellingly: competition for viewers is a strong motivating force. In Britain, for example, the competition between the evening news programmes on ITV and the BBC is well known. There is also a public demand for the news to be given in as short a time as possible. Some radio and television stations advertise the fact that they can give you the top stories in just 60 or even 30 seconds. Such everyday changes in language and style of communication happen gradually, and are therefore not always noticed. People accept the changes, get used to them and understand them.

By contrast with the secular media, in the same period of time – from the 1960s to the present – much of the language and style of communication of the church has not changed. A minority of people who attend church may be glad about that, but the majority of people find church boring, irrelevant and out of touch. This is the number one reason most people give for not attending church. What can be done to counteract this?

Changing the way the church communicates does not mean compromising its message. Dr Ravi Zacharias, speaking at the International Conference of Evangelists at Amsterdam 2000, said that for the twenty-first century,

> One of the disciplines will be that of learning to speak words that stir the imagination and demand the attention. We must recover the power of language once again. With the immersion into the visual and all the other ways we have of communicating, we must work hard at the very task of language and its beauty.

If the church fails to take into consideration changing styles and methods of communication, the result will be an increasing lack of effectiveness, further isolation from the community and declining congregations.

The communication gap

Communication is more than the mere transmission of information. Communication occurs when the message that is sent is understood in the way it was intended. There are three elements to the process: the content of the communication, the medium through which the message travels, and the recipient of the message. We shall be thinking about all three of these elements in the chapters which follow.

This book is mainly concerned with the communication of the gospel to the people who make up our local community. The majority of them have never attended church regularly and some have never entered a church in their lives. John

Drane, a theologian from Aberdeen University, addressing the Annual Baptist Assembly in the UK in 1999, said,

> One of the greatest tragedies facing the church is not that people in Britain are spiritually indifferent or anti-Christian, but precisely the opposite: they are spiritually searching, and open to the gospel, but are unable to hear it. For the most part, they can't hear it because we are not communicating the faith in ways that are accessible to anyone except ourselves.[1]

In an effort to connect with the general population, churchgoers are urged to be missionaries of the gospel. Sunday by Sunday, conference after conference, Christians are urged to 'go out into the world'. The reality is, however, that they are already there. It is only a very small minority who spend 24 hours a day, seven days a week, in a church environment. In many instances those who are in the workplace are making a difference and are a positive influence for good. Nevertheless, many others are silent and inactive, not sure what to do or say. The truth is, most Christians have not been equipped by the churches which have told them to 'go out'. It is seen as the answer to declining church attendance, but simply to 'go out' is not enough. It is what we do or say when we are out there that matters. 'We must discover new ways of being church in the twenty-first century,' we are told. Is that the answer? Or should we rediscover the way of being church in the time of the Acts of the Apostles?

The church in Acts had a double emphasis. Church members not only went out to where the people were, but they also brought them back in. To fulfil the Great Commission of Matthew 28:19–20, we must do more than obey the first part of that command of Christ,

---

[1] John Drane, quoted in the *Free Church Chronicle*, April 2001, p. 10.

Therefore go and make disciples of all nations, baptising them in the name of the Father and of the Son and of the Holy Spirit, and teaching them to obey everything I have commanded you. And surely I am with you always, to the very end of the age.

'Baptising' and 'teaching' mean incorporating people into the body of Christ, something which the church of the second half of the twentieth century did not do very well. From the follow-up of new converts after the mid-century Billy Graham crusades, to the follow-up of new converts from an Alpha course, for 50 years the church has found it difficult to incorporate new Christians into the local church family. Why?

Many churches struggle because they do not know how to close the communication gap between the church and the community in which it is placed. This is partly because the community has changed and the church has not. Even some church buildings project the message that we are part of a bygone age. These buildings can so easily convey the impression that we are falling apart, irrelevant and out of date.

Many congregations have accepted the fact that they are to see themselves at the beginning of the new century as 'missionary congregations'. Yet they find it hard actually to *be* missionary congregations. They find it hard to break out of the old mindset. This problem is closely related to the issue of communication. The vast majority of churches in the UK are talking to themselves Sunday by Sunday. It makes no difference whether the church is traditional, contemporary, charismatic or reformed: in most congregations they are talking to themselves. Some efforts to become seeker-centred or seeker-sensitive have worked, of course, but many others have failed, thereby making it difficult to try anything new again.

Theologians such as Emil Brunner and Hendrik Kraemar reminded us in the early twentieth century that we are in a missionary situation and that the gospel continually needs to be translated into contemporary terms. This is the task which we have not performed very well. In spite of a great deal of sincere effort on the part of concerned Christians, the great majority of the population are seldom confronted with the gospel through the normal work and witness of the church.

In the parable of the great banquet in Luke 14 and Matthew 22, Jesus focuses on God's invitation to 'come' to what he has prepared: 'Come, for everything is now ready' (Luke 14:17). Jesus uses an invitation to a banquet as a sign of God's grace. In the parable, the servants are commanded, 'Go out quickly into the streets and alleys of the town and bring in the poor, the crippled, the blind and the lame.' We have neglected the principle to 'bring in', and therefore many local churches have become places for believers, not unbelievers. We have neglected the need to invite people to 'come' into the family of God, i.e. the church. In the parable, everything was 'ready' for those who were to be invited. Often, our churches are not ready, and so we do not have the confidence, or see the need, to invite people to come. Again, the issue is poor and ineffective communication.

The church is reluctant to acknowledge this fact, and when we do sit down to consider how more people can be helped to hear what we profoundly believe to be the most important message in the world, we often fail to address the issue of communication. Many older Christians are honestly puzzled as to why more people do not understand the gospel. The problem is that most of the thinking about the communication of the gospel begins and ends with the idea that as long as it is proclaimed, it does not matter *how* it is proclaimed. Surely this does matter. Medium and style are essential elements of effective communication.

In Matthew 10:19–20 Jesus says to his followers,

But when they arrest you, do not worry about what to say or how to say it. At that time you will be given what to say, for it will not be you speaking, but the Spirit of your Father speaking through you.

Again, in John 12:49–50 Jesus says,

For I did not speak of my own accord, but the Father who sent me commanded me what to say and how to say it. I know that his command leads to eternal life. So whatever I say is just what the Father has told me to say.

Twice here we have the phrase 'what to say and how to say it'. These two statements in Matthew and John are intriguing, particularly the one in John. I compared different translations, went to the Greek text and checked numerous commentaries. The majority view is that Jesus intends a distinction between 'saying' and 'speaking'. The same distinction appears in John 8:43. That which he should 'say' was a matter of revelation, and that which he should 'speak' was the method in which he made the revelation, or content of the message, known. Clearly Jesus had no time for spin doctors, but it seems he did recognize the importance not only of *what* to say but *how* to say it.

Of course, it used to be argued, and still is argued in many places, that the preacher is unable to meet people with the gospel within the four walls of the local church. That cannot be correct. Once we accept that argument as true, we have been defeated. The command to 'go out' has a second part to it: we must also 'bring back'. As John Wesley knew, we have to go outside, but eventually, if our communication is effective, there has to be somewhere into which we can bring the new believers. Is that not why Wesley is known as the founder of the Methodist Church?

Incorporating new believers into the church family is a communication issue, since part of the problem for new believers is trying to understand the church. Where incorporation has been taken seriously, and efforts have been made to communicate with new believers as well as unbelievers, there are many examples of churches which are healthy and growing, and which are connecting successfully with their local community and culture.

The vital point is this: whether we are trying to reach the unchurched, disciple new Christians, or help established Christians to become missionary congregations, the issue of changing communication patterns must be addressed.

Changing language

Over a period of time, words can develop different meanings. This is the reason why we continually need new translations of the Bible. Many would argue that they like the old-style language better, and the Authorized, or King James, Version is often preferred by people in drama and the arts. The language may well lend itself to dramatic readings, but it is not the most effective way of communicating the Bible's message to the vast majority of people today. As James White comments, it spoke 'beautifully and effectively to seventeenth-century people. While still beautiful in its prose, it has lost much of its effectiveness as a translation.'[2] If the Authorized Version is used, it has to be explained. Some preachers prefer it precisely because it gives them something to explain, but they often end up merely explaining old words with present-day words, rather than offering helpful insights or valuable exposition. I once heard a preacher doing this with the Letter of James. He ended up saying only what the New International Version said.

---

[2] James White, *Rethinking the Church*, Baker Books, 2000, p. 82.

Newer translations of the Bible are a simple reminder of the way in which the church needs to update its language if it is to communicate effectively. We may prefer the style of the Authorized Version ourselves, but to help others understand the biblical message we need the newer translations. In the introduction to the New Living Translation, 1 Kings 2:10 is compared in three different versions of the Bible. In the Authorized Version the verse reads, 'So David slept with his fathers, and was buried in the city of David.' In the New International Version it reads, 'Then David rested with his fathers and was buried in the City of David.' In the New Living Translation it reads, 'Then David died and was buried in the City of David.' The NLT translators say they have translated the real meaning of the Hebrew idiom 'slept with his fathers' into contemporary English. This is an example of the way words and phrases have changed their meanings, not only across the centuries, but also during the one hundred years of the twentieth century.

Dr Colin Greene, Head of Theology and Public Policy at the Bible Society, said in the spring of 2001, 'The recovery of the Bible as the creative energising, liberating Word of God remains, as one would expect, high on our current agenda.'[3]

Not only have old words developed new meanings, but new words have been invented. Furthermore, new ways of putting words together have developed. Just try comparing the language of films from the 1940s with that used in the current box office hits. How we use words and put them together to make sentences has clearly changed.

Then there is the matter of political correctness, which also affects the language we use. The police, for example, have been banned from using the word 'homosexual' in case it causes offence. The new advice appeared in the 2001 updated edition of the *Policing Diversity Handbook*, which

---

[3] Colin Greene, *Transmission*, Bible Society, Spring 2001, p. 3.

was distributed to 35,000 Metropolitan Police officers. In 2000, a Greater Manchester Police guidebook banned terms such as 'love', 'pet' or 'dear', saying they could cause offence. The Police Federation said the changing nuances of language were 'a minefield' when it came to determining what could be offensive.

Many will agree that the media have heavily influenced the way we communicate, the United States media in particular. Many young people now use American phrases and terminologies without knowing where they come from. Some of them prefer to use the American language because of the way it is portrayed by the media and entertainment industry, as well as by modern business and commerce. In 1999 a survey of 2,000 people (the largest survey of its kind in Britain) revealed that two thirds of those under the age of 26 now pronounce 'schedule' the American way – with a hard 'c'. The survey also revealed a growing fondness among the young for saying 'vacation', and for stressing the first syllable in 'princess' rather than the second.

The BBC once issued a directive to all its journalists requesting them not to use American terms. Diapers, they said, were nappies, trash was rubbish and cookies were biscuits. They had no means of holding back the general tide of change, however. Many Americanisms are now used in everyday English conversations, including 'shades' (sunglasses), 'mall' (shopping centre), 'gas' (petrol), 'bathroom' (toilet), 'pants' (trousers), 'candy' (sweets), 'fries' (chips) and 'apartment' (flat). Having visited the United States approximately 50 times since first going there as a student in 1963, I have watched this process of change taking place. We may decry the trend, but like it or not, the English language has changed and is continuing to change because of this transatlantic influence. I should also say, for balance, that some British words have made their way into the American vocabulary. While we may use 'boutique' as a fashionable alternative to 'shop', for example, they use 'shop' as a trendy alternative to 'store'.

WAN2TLK? (Want to talk?)

The most recent and perhaps most rapid communication revolution has been brought about by the advent of mobile phones. Text-messaging has introduced us to an entirely new method of communication, and we have developed a whole new language for the purpose, using letters and symbols instead of complete words. For years we have been familiar with such shorthand terms as 'ASAP' (as soon as possible) or 'ETA' (estimated time of arrival), but e-mail and the mobile phone have taken this kind of communicating to a new level. For increasing numbers of people, especially the young, text-messaging is the smart way to communicate in the twenty-first century. It is the fastest growing service on every mobile phone network.

Text messaging operates on four simple principles:

1. Make words as short as possible (wd = would).
2. Use a letter instead of a whole word (r = are).
3. Use acronyms for longer phrases (DTRT = do the right thing).
4. Spell words however you want to, providing it makes them shorter (luv = love; sry = sorry).

To emphasize the point that this is a whole new language, there are now text-messaging dictionaries available, containing thousands of abbreviations and symbols. Many people just enjoy the fun of communicating in such a fast and simple way, of unravelling what has been said, or of finding new ways to say something. (Will spk 2ul8r = I will speak to you later.)

The mood of a message can be communicated by symbols

(emoticons): a shorthand way of explaining or elaborating on the meaning of the message. These emoticons are made up of punctuation marks on the phone's keypad. The basic smiley face is just a colon, a dash and a closed bracket, :-), and when it is rotated through 90 degrees it becomes a smile. Some of these symbols can be quite complicated, but are very familiar to text-messaging enthusiasts – e.g. :-)K- = I am wearing a shirt and tie; or :-(= I did not like that last statement, or I am upset.

As well as the fun and creativity in making pictures and jokes using the minimum number of characters, there is a more serious side to text-messaging. Surveys show that some men find it especially tempting to express their feelings this way, particularly in messages such as 'I love you' and 'I'm sorry'. Apparently members of the Muslim community have also used text-messaging to call people to prayer!

Speed merchants

Back in 1970 Alvin Toffler drew attention to our increasingly short-term world.[4] The pressure is on to report news in as short a time as possible. More and more people are interested in the facts rather than the process, in the 'what', 'when' and 'where' rather than the 'how' and 'why'. Journalism, particularly competitive journalism, is about the short-term rather than the long-term. People want to hear the news as it happens. 'Today's top stories', 'the latest news' and 'breaking news' are becoming familiar slogans of broadcasting companies around the world.

Television in particular has the capacity to speed up the communication process. Colin Morris, one-time Head of Religion at the BBC, says in his book *God-in-a-Box*,

---

[4] Alvin Toffler, *Future Shock*, Bodley Head, 1970.

I was a missionary on the Zambian Copperbelt in the 1960s when television arrived. An astonishing revolution occurred. Young Africans who, a few months before the television station was set up, were unable to read and got their information from village gossip, were soon aping the dress and mannerisms of US television characters with total naturalness. Tribesmen for whom the inhabitants of the next village were strangers began to discuss world affairs with a degree of sophistication that was startling. Whole cultures leap-frogged from pre-literate to post-literate stages of development without pausing to absorb the intermediate stage of book learning.[5]

I had a similar experience in Albania in the early 1990s. I visited the country soon after it opened its doors after 40 years as the world's first officially recognized atheist state. Television and communication generally with the outside world had been strictly controlled. Suddenly, not only were the borders with Greece and former Yugoslavia open, but the world of broadcasting had also become accessible. I remember sitting in an Albanian home watching *Dallas* and other Western television programmes. Albanians realized very quickly that there was another world beyond their own. They acquired a taste for Western-style living, going to the borders to bring back worn-out cars, broken washing machines and any other modern appliance that had reached the end of its life by Western standards. The communication of outside information through broadcasting was astonishingly rapid.

Modern communication is not only rapid, but also portable and private. Albanians had to queue for hours to use a public telephone. Now we find that the public telephone box is increasingly under threat. Most houses have telephones these days, and, with the development of the mobile phone, we have the perfect means of portable, private communication. Add to

[5] Colin Morris, *God-in-a-Box,* Hodder & Stoughton, 1984, p. 11.

this the Internet, with its vast amount of easily accessible information, plus e-mail and text-messaging, and it becomes possible for people around the world to communicate quickly, cheaply and privately. If the church is to have a positive influence in the world, it must take more than a passing interest in all the changes that have taken place in the way people communicate today.

In Genesis 1 'God spoke'. He spoke again in his Son: 'The Word became flesh and made his dwelling among us' (John 1:14). Psalm 19 tells us that 'the heavens declare the glory of God'.

Historically, the Christian message has been communicated in a rich variety of ways, through both verbal and non-verbal media. Sermons, liturgical action, ecclesiastical architecture, painting, stained-glass windows and mystery plays have all played their part. Printing made it possible for the Bible to be within the reach of everyone. We are not, therefore, asking for anything new when we make a plea for the church to revise its way of communicating the faith. The message does not change, but the method of communicating it does.

New methods of communicating are not always easy, and the church has often lagged behind in making use of modern technology. However, there have also been some remarkable pioneers. Back in the 1930s, J. Arthur Rank pioneered the use of films to teach and proclaim the Christian faith. This was a revolutionary idea. At the time, many religious people were against films and the cinema. William Booth set hymns to the tunes of pub songs, and J. Arthur Rank was similarly accused of using the devil's tools to promote the Christian faith. Nevertheless, he formed the Religious Film Society and films were offered to almost anyone who would show them – youth clubs, schools, women's meetings, churches. Rank's one passion was to promote Christianity. He believed that God had given him the job of making good quality religious films. In order to show the films, of course, churches needed projectors. The Methodist Cinema Committee was formed to enable participating churches to hire a 16-millimetre sound projector for just £20 per year.

Then came the advent of television, and churches faced a new challenge. In 1965 the Revd Leslie Timmins, the first Director of CTVC, formerly known as the Churches Television Centre, challenged the churches to take seriously the opportunities provided by broadcasting: 'Without doubt these media provide an unparalleled opportunity for the proclamation of the Christian faith, if they are taken seriously by the Church.'[6] He recalled that on Christmas Eve 1922, the first religious address was broadcast, to be followed in January 1924 by the first radio broadcast worship service, which came from St Martin-in-the-Fields, London.

Today the Christian presence on *mainstream* radio and television is diminishing. There are fewer broadcast worship services, live or recorded. Why? Because audiences are dropping. Why are audiences dropping? Not only because fewer people may be interested in Christianity, but also because the church is no longer communicating effectively. Is that why we face a situation of declining church attendance? Where the church does communicate effectively, demonstrating the excitement and relevance of the Christian faith today, worship attendance increases. Likewise, where a religious programme communicates effectively, be it a broadcast worship service, a magazine-style programme or a documentary, it is possible to sustain larger audiences. Recent examples of such success in the UK include the series broadcast on ITV in December 2000 called *Bethlehem Year Zero*, and the three-part series *Son of God* shown on BBC1 before Easter 2001.

---

[6] Leslie Timmins, *Vision On*, Epworth Press, 1965, p. 97.

I close this chapter as I began, with reference to Ravi Zacharias, who commented at Amsterdam 2000 on the present-day 'dominance of the visual'. He talked about the 'staggering impact of the visual. The medium of entertainment has become the shaper of a generation's way of thinking.' But he went on to point out,

> There is another side to this, and we should not forget it. Just because this generation thinks visually does not mean they do not think deeply. They do, about the issues that trouble them. Our expression was in words. Young people often do it in symbols, and they are just as deep.

The question is, how do you reach a generation that hears with its eyes and thinks with its feelings?

2

In Times of Spiritual Awakening

As I mentioned in the previous chapter, there are three elements to the process of communication: the content of the
communication, the medium through which that content
travels, and the recipient of the content. In this chapter we
will see how all three elements have been present in times of
authentic Christian spiritual awakening.

The content

Historically, at the heart of times of spiritual revival has been
the rediscovery of the biblical message of faith, hope and love.

> As far as Christians are concerned, the message is given. There
> is no question of our inventing a fresh one to suit the appetites
> of our time or of our media. But from the riches of that message
> it is necessary to select that aspect of its truth which is relevant
> to a particular recipient on a particular occasion.[1]

This was said by a friend of mine who was a broadcaster
for many years, long before the phrase 'seeker-centred' was
heard in the UK. He continued,

---

[1] Peter Brooks, *Communicating Conviction*, Epworth Press, 1983, p. 10.

Neither the medium nor the listener can dictate what Christianity is, but they have a right to be offered it in forms which match up to both. The apostle Paul was no trimmer, but he was ready to become all things to all men in order to save some of them.

In times of spiritual renewal and awakening the message has always been dominant. In the Acts of the Apostles, the disciples faithfully and effectively evangelized their world. Since those days, during times of awakening, the content of the message has never changed. The words have changed with the times and the circumstances, the message has often been rediscovered, but it has never changed. Effective Christian communicators have never compromised the message. They have always preached for a verdict. They have not hesitated to confront people with the claims of Jesus Christ and the need for a deliberate decision. There is, however, a need to be flexible and creative in Christian communication: the message may not change, but the strategies must.

John Chrysostom (AD 347–407), a man regarded by many as one of the greatest preachers in the history of the church and often referred to as 'golden mouth', built his preaching on five principles:[2]

1. An excellent knowledge of the Bible.
2. A good command of language.
3. A compassionate heart for people.
4. An ability to relate theology to everyday life.
5. A passionate enthusiasm when preaching.

We will look at those principles more fully later, but in this chapter let us take to heart the first principle, 'an excellent

---

[2] *Baptist Leader*, Issue No. 14, Summer 1996, BUGB.

knowledge of the Bible'. For 2,000 years the authority and centrality of the Bible has been key to effective Christian communication. When the truth of the Bible is related to human needs, people become interested. The word of God is powerful in the hands of the Holy Spirit; it produces faith on the part of hearers; it becomes a source of guidance, wisdom, assurance and hope for the future; it encourages, comforts and challenges; it transforms lives and builds people up in their relationship with God and with others.

In the fifteenth century, a dejected monk retreated to his tiny cell and gave himself to the study of the Scriptures. The message of the Bible came alive to him, and he preached 300 sermons from the book of Revelation in St Mark's Cathedral in Florence, Italy. The preaching of Savonarola brought about a time of rich spiritual awakening. It was the result of the Holy Spirit working through a willing and sur-rendered communicator, but an essential ingredient of the process was the uncompromised message of the Bible.

Other great communicators followed Savonarola, such as Luther, Calvin and Zwingli. The authority of the Bible was rediscovered through the lives and ministries of such preach-ers. These are examples of how, when the message of the Bible is proclaimed in the power of the Holy Spirit, tremen-dous things happen. Cultures are changed, lives are changed, churches are renewed and awakened.

In the eighteenth century, the preaching of Jonathan Edwards changed the course of North American history. There were many other preachers during this time, in what was called the First Great Awakening. Among them was George Whitefield from Britain, who sailed across the Atlantic many times. He was a contemporary of John Wesley, and both men were mightily used in the British Great Awakening.

In the late 1870s another great surge of revival swept the newly formed United States of America: 'As the First

Awakening had its beginnings among New England Congregationalists and Presbyterians, the Second Awakening broke out in Methodist and Baptist circles in Virginia and soon spread to the Carolinas.'[3]

The nineteenth century saw another awakening. This time, a brilliant 29-year-old barrister became the channel of communication. He was Charles Finney, pastor, teacher and social reformer. Whole cities were changed under the impact of his preaching. Finney preached with great clarity and power. It was once said of him that he explained what others preach about. The nineteenth-century awakening also launched the powerful and effective evangelistic ministry of D. L. Moody.

At the same time as all of this was happening in North America, there was once more a counterpart movement in Britain, and this revival had great social impact. William Wilberforce, who was a product of the revival, was the famous parliamentarian who pioneered the abolition of slavery.

In the second half of the nineteenth century, London was greatly influenced by the preaching of Charles Haddon Spurgeon. Spurgeon became widely known as an educator and a philanthropist, but most of all as a preacher. He began preaching as a teenager. Still just a young man, he came to London and preached at New Park Street Baptist Church. He had an immediate impact. When the morning service ended, 'the impressed congregation – only eighty in number – filed out. That afternoon the good members fanned out over south London inviting friends to the evening service. A large congregation gathered in the evening.'[4] Spurgeon soon

---

[3] Lewis Drummond, *The Awakening That Must Come*, Broadman Press, 1978, p. 15.

[4] Lewis and Betty Drummond, *Women of Awakenings*, Kregel Publications, 1997, p. 147.

began to build up the congregation, both spiritually and numerically, and went on to preach to tens of thousands in the course of his ministry.

What was the secret of Spurgeon's effectiveness? He both believed and explained the Bible. On the 18th March 1855, while preaching from the Old Testament book of Hosea, Spurgeon expressed his view of the Bible and his confidence in its message. He said, 'This is the book untainted by any error; but is pure, unalloyed, perfect truth. Why? Because God wrote it.'

Commenting on Spurgeon's statement and similar statements made by others from those days, Lewis Drummond says, 'The various books of the Bible obviously reflect the vocabulary, grammatical and writing ability, sociological and historical conditions, theological viewpoints, and intent of the various writers.'[5] Yet, as Professor A. T. Robertson has pointed out, the Bible is 'a supernatural revelation above reason which reason never could have obtained unless it had come in this way'.[6] It is not the purpose of this book to enter the debate concerning the reliability of different translations of the Bible, or of Scripture generally, but simply to make the point that the most effective communicators of the Christian faith have a strong confidence in the Bible as God's message to humankind.

Lack of confidence in the Bible as the message of God inevitably creates a crisis of communication for the preacher. Historically, there has been no spiritual awakening when such a lack of confidence existed. This point is well illustrated in the early life of the twentieth-century evangelist Billy Graham.

Just before the famous Los Angeles crusade of 1949,

---

[5] Lewis Drummond, *The Word of the Cross*, Broadman, 1992, pp. 51–52.
[6] A. T. Robertson, *The Relative Authority of Scripture and Reason*, quoted by Drummond in *Word of the Cross*, p. 65.

Graham was in the thick of a spiritual battle. His friend Chuck Templeton had long had doubts about the integrity of the Bible, and the two men met for hours of debate and prayer. As they debated, Graham became increasingly confused. Could he continue to accept the authority of the Bible in the face of problems apparently too difficult to resolve? Months went by, and the Los Angeles crusade drew nearer. Graham was unwell, with what he called a 'terrific pain at the base of my skull'. He was tired and tense. John Pollock takes up the story.

> Billy went out in the forest and wandered up the mountain, praying as he walked, 'Lord, what shall I do? What shall be the direction of my life?' He saw that intellect alone could not resolve the question of authority. He must go beyond intellect. 'So I went back and got my Bible, and I went out in the moonlight. And I got to a stump and put the Bible on the stump, and I knelt down, and I said, "Oh God; I cannot prove certain things. I cannot answer some of the questions Chuck is raising and some of the other people are raising, but I accept this Book by faith as the Word of God."'[7]

Graham went on to the Los Angeles crusade, which became the watershed for his future ministry.

For several decades in the twentieth century, Billy Graham was known for his familiar phrase, 'the Bible says'. His conviction that he could trust the integrity of the Bible led him to say just before his famous London crusades in the 1950s,

> I am going to present a God who matters, and who makes claims on the human race. He is a God of love, grace and mercy, but also a God of judgement. When we break his moral laws we suffer; when we keep them, we have inward peace and joy. I am

---

[7] John Pollock, *Billy Graham*, McGraw-Hill, 1966, p. 53.

going to insist that honesty and integrity pay in individual lives. I am calling for a revival that will cause men and women to return to their offices and shops to live out the teaching of Christ in their daily relationships. I am going to preach a gospel not of despair but of hope – hope for the individual, for society and for the world.[8]

History shows that during times of authentic spiritual revival, the Bible's message changes the lives of many people.

In 1936, Professor C. H. Dodd wrote a small book which became a classic, *Apostolic Preaching and Its Development*. In this book, Dodd makes a distinction between the two Greek words *didaskein* and *kerygma*. The first he defines as teaching, i.e. ethical and moral instructions on the Christian life. The second is preaching, i.e. 'public proclamation of Christianity to the non-Christian world'.[9] As far back as the first half of the twentieth century, Dodd was saying that much of the preaching in the contemporary church would not have been recognized by the first Christians as *kerygma*.

For the early church, then, to preach the gospel was by no means the same thing as to deliver moral instruction or exhortation. While the church was concerned to hand on the teaching of the Lord, it was not by this that it made converts. It was by *kerygma*, said Paul . . . that it pleased God to save men.[10]

Dodd draws a distinction, therefore, between teaching and preaching. Teaching is an essential ministry of the Christian church. There are Christian women and men who are gifted as teachers. Teaching, however, is not necessarily preaching, although preaching may contain some teaching.

---

[8] Ibid., p. 118.
[9] C. H. Dodd, *Apostolic Preaching and Its Development*, Hodder & Stoughton, 1936, p. 7.
[10] Ibid., p. 78.

The best biblical example of preaching is Peter's message in Acts 2. It contains information, but it also contains persuasion and a clear call to change: 'Then Peter continued preaching for a long time, strongly urging all his listeners, "Save yourselves from this generation that has gone astray!"' (Acts 2:40 NLT).

Preaching is exhortation. It is a unique method of communication. The apostle Paul says in 1 Corinthians 1:21 that God 'was pleased through the foolishness of what was preached to save those who believe'. Indeed, there is a foolishness about preaching that is not necessarily present in teaching. Biblical preaching is the story of Jesus Christ. As Paul says, it is 'the message of the cross'.

A summary of *kerygma* – the message of the gospel to the non-Christian world – is provided by Lewis Drummond in the account of Peter's sermon on the Day of Pentecost in Acts 1 and 2.

1. Jesus Christ of Nazareth is the fulfilment of Old Testament prophecies concerning the coming of God's kingdom and salvation through his Messiahship (Acts 2:16–21).
2. Jesus is the incarnate Son of God (Acts 2:22).
3. Jesus lived a sinless, revealing, perfect life doing many glorious miracles (Acts 2:22).
4. Jesus Christ was crucified on the cross to make atonement for the sin of the world (Acts 2:23).
5. Jesus Christ was raised bodily from the dead, thereby triumphing over sin, death, hell and the grave (Acts 2:24), and ascended into heaven to be at the Father's right hand (Acts 1:9).
6. Jesus Christ is coming again to usher in the fullness of the kingdom (Acts 1:11).
7. People are called to repent, believe and follow Christ in commitment to life, as symbolized in baptism (Acts 2:38).

8. The person who responds receives the promise of forgiveness of sins (Acts 2:38).
9. That person also receives the gift of the Holy Spirit (Acts 2:38).
10. A whole new life is experienced by the person who responds (Acts 2:42).

Today we have one other important aspect to consider. The twenty-first-century church is called to proclaim the gospel in an increasingly pluralistic world. At Amsterdam 2000, the International Conference for Evangelists organized by the Billy Graham Association, the content of the evangelist's message was discussed. The point was made that because God's general revelation extends to all points of his creation, there are traces of truth, beauty and goodness in many non-Christian belief systems. As we enter into dialogue with people of other faiths, we must be courteous and kind. Evangelists were urged to treat those of other faiths with respect and to serve our nations faithfully in an attitude of humility, while affirming that Christ is the one and only Saviour of the world.

The medium

In times of spiritual awakening, God has used unusual women and men as vehicles of his message. In the Old Testament, for example, there is Deborah, who has been described as 'the prophetess of awakening'. In the New Testament, Priscilla was powerfully used by God. Tertullian, one of the early church fathers, records, 'By the holy Prisca [Priscilla], the gospel is preached.' Priscilla is the Deborah of the New Testament. In Acts 18:23–26 we see how she impacted the life of the preacher Apollos. In later history, God used women such as Madam Guyon in France, Catherine Booth of the Salvation Army, Amy Carmichael in

India, and, more recently, Anne Graham Lotz, daughter of the evangelist Billy Graham, who has become a powerful preacher in her own right. As for the men, God has used great figures such as Martin Luther, John Wesley, William Carey, William Booth, Charles Spurgeon, Dwight L. Moody, Billy Graham and many others.

What is it that these men and women have in common as communicators? First, they all have a strong commitment to God. They are men and women of purpose. They have a deep awareness of God. They also have an awareness of their call to mission. Their spirituality is central to them, and they have a keen sense of dependence on God. They recognize that what they have in terms of effectiveness comes as a gift from God and is not of their own making. They are men and women of genuine humility. They are not all extroverts, but include many different temperaments and types of personality. However, their characters are shaped by God, and he makes use of their different personalities.

Phillips Brooks, the nineteenth-century bishop, in his famous book *Lectures on Preaching*, says that preaching is the communication of truth by men and women to men and women. It has 'two essential elements, truth and personality. Neither of those can it spare and still be preaching.' He argues that truth,

> communicated in any other way than through the personality of the communicator is not preached truth. On the other hand, if they use their powers of persuasion or of entertainment to make others listen to their speculations, or do their will, or applaud their cleverness, that is not preaching either. The first lacks personality. The second lacks truth.[11]

The point is that God equips those whom he calls, those who are willing to be totally committed and who will not

---

[11] Phillips Brooks, *Lectures on Preaching*, Allenson, 1902, p. 5.

compromise that commitment. They are often described as 'true men and women of God', 'godly', 'Christ-like', 'people of integrity'. They are communicators who are transparent, authentic and genuinely modest characters.

Second, they are gifted in unusual ways. Physically, intellectually and emotionally, they are equipped for the task. It was said of Spurgeon that he had a voice 'as clear as a bell' that could be heard easily by vast audiences, without the help of today's sound systems. Billy Graham had a quality of voice that expressed genuine warmth for and empathy with his listeners. He also had clear diction.

Third, they express their message in the language of the day, clearly, simply and with great conviction. They have the ability to express deep truths in simple ways. It is hard to express deep spiritual realities in simple terms without being shallow, but these gifted communicators get it right. Phillips Brooks makes a telling observation in which he says,

> It has often seemed to me as if the vast amount of preaching which people hear must have one bad effect, in leaving on their minds a vague impression that this Christian life to which they are so essentially urged must be a very difficult and complicated thing that it should take such a multitude of definitions to make it clear.[12]

Times have not changed.

The recipient

Is it more difficult to capture the attention of people today than it was hundreds of years ago, before the age of mass broadcasting? Many would argue that it is. Nonetheless, people will still respond to a message that connects with their interests, their fears and their future.

---

[12] Ibid., p. 2.

Matching the message and the medium to this third factor demands a lot of human understanding combined with some knowledge of the psychological and sociological factors which condition human responses.[13]

All too often, Christian communicators are answering questions that have not been asked, and are speaking in a language which is not understood, or in places where nobody is listening. Not so with those who have been used in times of spiritual awakening. They connected with their audiences. Their preaching touched people in the circumstances and situations in which they were living.

> For communication is more than mere transmission, it is more than mere proclamation. You and I have an inescapable responsibility to ensure as much as it lies within our power to do so, that the message we send is understood in the way we intended. The evangelist communicates effectively, when the message delivered is understood clearly enough to be used of God to bring conviction to the hearer's heart.[14]

This is what the communicators in times of moral and spiritual awakening were able to do, and we need to do it again.

Peter Brooks, a respected BBC broadcaster and religious producer, said nearly 20 years ago, 'We need to speak to their felt needs in such a way as to reach through them to deeper needs than ever they have been aware of.' An example of this in a time of spiritual awakening was the preacher Jonathan Edwards in his famous sermon, 'Sinners in the Hands of an Angry God'. Although we may not use such a sermon title on a church noticeboard today, Edwards preached with great persuasion to win people to Christ. Powerfully moved by the

---

[13] Peter Brooks, *Communicating Conviction*, p. 11.
[14] Gerry Gallimore at Amsterdam 2000.

Holy Spirit, he touched people's lives at a point of need deeper than they knew.

Rick Warren, a highly effective present-day communicator who, in 20 years, saw his church grow from two people to 22,000 in Orange County, California, says, 'Every week I begin with a need, hurt, or interest and then move to what God has to say about it in his Word.' He continues,

> Preaching to felt needs is scorned and criticized in some circles as a cheapening of the Gospel and a sellout to consumerism. I want to state this in the clearest way possible: Beginning a message with people's felt needs is more than a marketing tool! It is based on the theological fact that God chooses to reveal himself to [us] according to *our* needs! Both the Old and New Testaments are filled with examples of this. Even the names of God are revelations of how God meets our felt needs.[15]

There is great suspicion about preaching to 'felt needs', but all that means is starting where people are and addressing the issues they understand. 'Every good teacher knows to start with the students' interests and move them toward the lesson to be studied.'[16]

Billy Graham had a sermon called 'The Value of the Soul'. He preached it at least five times across five decades: 1957 in New York, 1968 in Portland, Oregon, 1977 in Cincinnati, 1986 in Washington DC, and 1997 in San Jose, California. The content of the sermon stayed the same, but the delivery and style of presentation changed. There were two reasons for this. Obviously Billy himself was changing; he was maturing. More importantly, the culture was changing; people's perceptions were changing; the way people listened was changing – and he knew it and adapted.

Communication has played a vital role in spiritual

---

[15] Rick Warren, *The Purpose-Driven Church*, Zondervan, 1995, p. 295.
[16] Ibid., p. 225.

awakening, in the days of the Old Testament, during the birth of the church recorded in the New Testament book of Acts, and right through the centuries to the present day. Wherever authentic spiritual revival has occurred, effective communication and gifted communicators have been at the heart of those awakenings.

3

Jesus the Master Communicator

Jesus is our model for communication. He is the master communicator. In Mark 1:14–15 we read,

> After John was put in prison, Jesus went into Galilee, proclaiming the good news of God. 'The time has come,' he said. 'The kingdom of God is near. Repent and believe the good news!'

Later in that same chapter we read of the purpose of Jesus' mission.

> Very early in the morning, while it was still dark, Jesus got up, left the house and went off to a solitary place, where he prayed. Simon and his companions went to look for him, and when they found him, they exclaimed: 'Everyone is looking for you!'
> Jesus replied, 'Let us go somewhere else – to the nearby villages – so I can preach there also. That is why I have come.' So he travelled throughout Galilee, preaching in their synagogues. (vv. 35–39)

Notice that Jesus says, 'That is why I have come.' His whole purpose was to proclaim the gospel of God. In his preaching, his actions, his life, death and resurrection, Jesus was seeking to communicate the good news of God. Of

47

course, we cannot overlook the impact of his life, death and resurrection, but for the purpose of this chapter, we must concentrate on his preaching. Nonetheless, effective communication cannot be separated from character and lifestyle, and we will look at this further in later chapters.

One might say that communication is amoral. In other words, a good communicator does not necessarily bring good news. It may seem that way at first, of course – perhaps the twentieth-century example of Hitler is a case in point. In total contrast, Jesus came openly proclaiming 'good news'. Truly effective communication can always be measured by the question, 'Does it last?' Does the message, when fully understood, go on impacting people's lives in a healthy way?

Jesus was undoubtedly an effective communicator: we are told that 'the large crowd listened to him with delight' (Mark 12:37). Mark also tells us that 'large crowds . . . followed him'. Twenty-three times in the first three Gospels, 'crowds' are referred to as following Jesus. In all four Gospels the word 'crowd' in connection with the ministry of Jesus is used no less than 99 times. People do not gather in crowds around an individual unless that individual, or his or her life, has something to say. Not everyone in the crowd understood or even agreed with Jesus – many hated him and his message – and some who 'listened to him with delight' did not always act on his message. Yet the fact remains, from the evidence of the Gospels, that Jesus was a master communicator.

Every reader of the New Testament will realize that Jesus used lots of stories to communicate his message; stories which have become instilled in people's minds without them always knowing where they came from. Stories such as those about the Prodigal Son and the Good Samaritan are so powerfully clear in their message that, once told, they seem hardly to be forgotten. The stories are simple and very visual. Who could read those stories without picturing the open arms of the father welcoming home his returning son, or seeing the beaten traveller lying by the side of the road with the Samaritan bending over him in compassion? Martin Luther King gave a sermon on the Good Samaritan which began, 'I should like to talk to you about a good man, whose exemplary life will always be a flashing light to plague the dozing conscience of mankind.'[1] That is exactly why Jesus' simple story of a man who was a good neighbour will always be remembered.

If we ask, 'What is Jesus best known for?' the answer among those who know something about him would probably be three things:

> First, the circumstances of his birth and death (thanks to the post-card manufacturers, we all know that he was placed in a manger at Christmas and died on a cross at Easter!); next that he had a reputation for performing miracles; and lastly, that he spoke in parables.[2]

Jesus used parables or stories when he was preaching to the crowds. It is a precedent we would do well to follow. He also linked his parables to the environment and circumstances of the people who were listening. Through those parables, Jesus showed that he had enormous insight into human nature, and the stories speak to men and women in every age. It is this timeless quality that causes them to be remembered. These vivid stories find an extraordinary echo in the hearts and minds of people in any century.

Jesus was using his parables to teach people about the nature of the kingdom of God, the conditions of entry into the kingdom, and the consummation of the kingdom. He taught deep truth in simple ways – something many modern

---

[1] Martin Luther King, *Strength to Love*, Fontana, 1969, p. 26.

[2] George Beasley-Murray, *Preaching the Gospel from the Gospels*, Epworth Press, 1965, p. 102.

preachers and Christian communicators find very difficult to do. It takes much more hard work and discipline. My experience with broadcasting has taught me that it is far more demanding to prepare an 8-minute sermon than a 20- or 30-minute one. In the 8-minute sermon, every sentence must count. There is no scope for wasted words. Some preachers I know will not submit to that kind of discipline, and thereby forfeit their opportunity to communicate effectively to large numbers of people.

This brings us back not only to what Jesus said, but to how he said it. Jesus' words from John 12:49–50 are worth repeating:

> For I did not speak of my own accord, but the Father who sent me commanded me what to say and how to say it. I know that his command leads to eternal life. So whatever I say is just what the Father has told me to say.

How we express ourselves is always important. How we say something can easily contradict what we say. We probably know the old phrase, 'I can't hear what you're saying because who you are speaks so loudly.'

How we say something can also attract people to what we say. A well-known preacher in the first half of the twentieth century who was well ahead of his day was Peter Marshall, the Minister of New York Avenue Presbyterian Church, Washington DC. He was a Scotsman, which may have given him some advantage in the USA, but his effectiveness was not just down to his accent. He was a gifted communicator who brought the Bible stories to life in such a powerful way that people queued six deep to get into the church. Catherine Marshall recalls the kind of effect he had.

> A tired Washington radio newscaster, who had to rise at 5.30 each Sunday morning and work until four o'clock, started coming to New York Avenue for the Sunday evening service. He

reported, 'The first Sunday I heard Dr Marshall I knew nothing at all about him or his background. I wondered how I was going to stay awake, but during the sermon I forgot my fatigue. I marvelled at his clear diction. At first my attention was held completely by the *way* this man was saying things. Then my interest shifted rapidly to *what* he was saying . . . It was obvious that God was near and real to him. He used vivid word-pictures . . . His wonderful speaking ability, his power of expression – I found out as time went on – always seemed to reach its greatest height in the Lenten season. He could describe Christ, the disciples, the events and persons around them, as graphically as a special-events broadcaster on the scene . . .'[3]

It was who Jesus was, as well as what he said, that drew large crowds. He preached with compassion. He addressed the issues of the day. He challenged injustice and exploitation. He loved and accepted the tired, the weary, the marginalized, whether they were poor or rich. He understood where people were coming from spiritually.

Exactly how Jesus preached, we cannot be sure. Obviously he said far more than we have recorded for us in the four Gospels, but however condensed they might be, there is enough in the Gospels to give us some strong pointers. Jesus clearly communicated not only with words, but also with his eyes and with his touch. When he looked at Peter, after Peter's bitter denial, the look that passed between them spoke volumes. More than one artist has tried to capture what might have been the expression on Jesus' face at that moment. Luke tells the story with particular feeling. Peter was in the process of denying all friendship with Jesus:

Just as he was speaking, the cock crowed. The Lord turned and looked straight at Peter. Then Peter remembered the word the

---

Lord had spoken to him: 'Before the cock crows today, you will disown me three times.' And he went outside and wept bitterly. (Luke 22:60–62)

Jesus also touched many people, and allowed people to touch him. When he touched the leper, Jesus communicated love and compassion in such a way that to this day the story still holds attention whenever it is told.

Even if we cannot know in detail what it was like to hear Jesus preaching, therefore, we can learn much from the Gospels which is directly relevant to today's need for effective communication.

1. Jesus spoke with authority

Early in Mark's Gospel we read, 'The people were amazed at his teaching, because he taught them as one who had authority, not as the teachers of the law' (Mark 1:22). The authority of Jesus is mentioned no less than 34 times in the four Gospels, either by the Gospel writers or by the crowds and individuals to whom Jesus was speaking. He spoke with strength and influence. There must have been conviction in his voice and manner.

We cannot present truth in a listless and lazy way. Unless people sense that we genuinely long for them to know God, to feel his love and experience his forgiveness, we shall have little influence. There was no bland, boring presentation with Jesus. He was arresting, exciting, pointed, penetrating, compelling and, of course, anointed by God. To become passionate and persuasive communicators, we too must spend time with God. Our authority comes from him alone. We must not only spend time honing our communication skills, but we must consciously seek the presence of God, get to know him better, and ask for his power through the Holy Spirit.

2. Jesus was creative in his communication

Jesus was flexible, always aware of the audience he was addressing. The apostle Paul learned from this.

> To the weak I became weak, to win the weak. I have become all things to all men so that by all possible means I might save some. I do all this for the sake of the gospel, that I may share in its blessings. (1 Corinthians 9:22–23)

Gerry Gallimore, a pastor speaking at the International Conference for Evangelists in Amsterdam in the summer of 2000, put it this way:

> We must take time to get to know our audience, to find the common ground, to understand the point of entry to their hearts, so that we communicate saving truth in terms they understand and can identify with.
>
> Jesus was a master at this. Watch him as he called the disciples to follow him. He told them he would make them 'fishers of men' (Matt. 4:19). That did it. That kind of language immediately resonated with these Galilean fishermen. Watch him with farmers, he spoke to them about sowing and reaping, and about weeds and wheat; with the woman at the well, it was about water. With Zaccheus, it was business terms; with Pilate it was political language. The words and examples that Jesus used were filled with imagery familiar to the people he addressed. To be effective we must follow his example!

3. Jesus spoke with simplicity and directness

The Sermon on the Mount is the ultimate example: what could be clearer, simpler, more direct than 'Love your enemies and pray for those who persecute you'?

Is there anything vague about that? Or, 'When you pray, go into your room, close the door and pray to your Father, who is unseen.' Is there anything unclear about that? Or, 'If you forgive those who sin against you, your heavenly Father will forgive you.' Can anything be more direct than that? Or, 'Do for others what you would like them to do for you.' Is there anything complicated about that?

At the end of the sermon, recorded in Matthew, Jesus tells the highly visual story of the two builders. Any builder, then or today, would recognize immediately the importance of building on a firm foundation and not on a soft one. The application is totally clear. To get through life we must build our lives on principles and values that are going to last – i.e., on a good foundation. The illustration is simple, clear and memorable. 'After Jesus finished speaking, the crowds were amazed at his teaching, for he taught as one who had real authority – quite unlike the teachers of religious law' (Matthew 7:28–29 NLT).

Jesus spoke clearly and with power. His words stimulated a response in people. The response was not always positive, but his listeners were not sleeping through his sermons, nor were they indifferent. Jesus' preaching allowed men and women to see God and the kind of relationship they had with him. His simple delivery motivated people to hear him.

We can see from Jesus' example that to be simple you do not have to be shallow. You do not have to compromise the message. How different that is from much preaching today. Many modern Christian communicators, both writers and preachers, seem to believe that unless they are complicated they cannot be profound. For some, it may even be pride that prevents them from the discipline of teaching deep truth in simple ways.

4. Jesus often used single statements to convey his message

So far I have resisted saying that Jesus was a master of the soundbite, but in fact, according to the Gospel writers, he was. The Gospel writers show Jesus delivering sentences that conveyed huge truths, using the minimum of words. 'I am the light of the world.' 'I am the Good Shepherd.' 'I am the way, the truth and the life.' When talking about others, he said, 'You are the light of the world.' 'You are the salt of the earth.' Not only do these single statements convey deep truths, but they are easy to remember. People always remember sentences more easily than paragraphs. The effectiveness of many of Jesus' sayings is clear from the fact that they are often quoted by people who have very little knowledge of the Bible or church. They are heard in the most unlikely contexts. They sometimes even appear in advertisements.

The Gospel writers also record what has become known as 'The Lord's Prayer' – the prayer that Jesus taught his disciples. It has few words. There may have been more to this prayer originally, but that does not alter the fact that what is recorded is remarkably brief and yet full of meaning. Whole books have been written about the Lord's Prayer, but how few words there are in the prayer itself. Every sentence is rich with meaning. Not a word is wasted. This is in sharp contrast to much modern-day preaching and communication, which often contains such long sentences and convoluted thinking that it is easy to forget at the end what was said at the beginning. One of the advantages of preaching from a full script, incidentally, is that you can easily identify any long sentences which can then be cut down to a more manageable size.

Not many of us can preach sermons that are remembered the following week, but it is possible to make key statements that actually say something, and that may well be remembered. Personally, I always try to sum up a sermon in a single sentence. If I cannot say in a single sentence what the sermon is about, how will anyone else understand it or remember the main point? For example, if I am preaching a series of messages based on Psalm 23, I will use such titles as 'How do I handle the dark valleys of life?' In a single sentence, people know what the sermon is going to be about.

5. Jesus preached for a verdict

Jesus called people to action. The Sermon on the Mount is full of calls to action, as are his shorter messages recorded in the Gospels. Jesus did not just convey information. He called for commitment. He challenged people to change their thinking, to change their attitudes, to change their lifestyles. At the end of the Sermon on the Mount, which is almost entirely application, Jesus says, 'Everyone who hears these words of mine *and puts them into practice* is like a wise man who built his house on the rock' (Matthew 7:24, italics mine).

The clearest example of Jesus preaching for a verdict is recorded in Mark 8:34–35.

> Then he called the crowd to him along with his disciples and said: 'If anyone would come after me, he must deny himself and take up his cross and follow me. For whoever wants to save his life will lose it, but whoever loses his life for me and for the gospel will save it.'

Jesus called people to change. To Nicodemus, he said, 'You must be born again.' To the woman caught in the act of adultery, Jesus said, 'Go now and leave your life of sin.' To the paralytic in Mark 2:9–11, he said, 'I tell you, get up, take your mat and go home.'

Sometimes in a gentle, compassionate manner, sometimes in a confrontational and challenging way, Jesus called people to change direction. He did not expect people to stay the same. This is clear from the very beginning of his ministry, according to Mark, who records Jesus preaching, 'The time has come . . . The kingdom of God is near. Repent and believe the good news!' Repentance means a change of direction. Right from the beginning of his ministry, Jesus called for a verdict. 'Who do people say I am?' he asked (Mark 8:27). Even in the exchange between Pilate and Jesus, just by being in front of Pilate, Jesus was calling for a change.

Pilate then went back inside the palace, summoned Jesus and asked him, 'Are you the king of the Jews?'

'Is that your own idea,' Jesus asked, 'or did others talk to you about me?' (John 18:33–34)

Jesus did not simply pass out information. He said, 'I have come that they may have life, and have it to the full' (John 10:10). He did not preach just for the sake of helping people to be better informed, he preached so that their lives might be changed.

So often we can be the exact opposite to Jesus. Instead of calling for action, we can leave people with an uncertainty about what has been said. Responsible theology is vital, but we can be so preoccupied with it that people leave church unclear about what action they should take. We avoid the discipline of simplicity and directness. We give in to the temptation to dress up basic truths to sound complex. We may be more concerned about making a good impression than about being an agent of change, and so we lack conviction and authority.

The number one reason most people give for leaving church is that they have been put off by boring, irrelevant preaching. Having seen the gap between the creative communication of Jesus and our own efforts, what can we do to become more effective communicators of God's grace?

PART 2

The Spoken Word

4

The Role of Preaching

I sat in church one Sunday morning and watched both preacher and congregation. The sermon contained good material, but failed to connect with the congregation because of the monotonous style and language in which the message was delivered. People were lulled into a state of semi-attentiveness. One lady was picking bobbles of wool from the sleeves of her cardigan. A man stared at the floor in front of him.

If the Bible continues to capture the imaginations of film producers, television directors and music writers, why can it not capture the imagination of more preachers? If it did, it would be far more likely to capture the imagination of congregations as well. Yet sometimes we turn the most exciting, positive and relevant book in the world into one which bores people. Rick Warren points out,

> When God's word is taught in an uninteresting way, people don't just think the pastor is boring, they think God is boring! We slander God's character if we preach with an uninspiring style or tone.[1]

---

[1] Rick Warren, *The Purpose-Driven Church*, Zondervan, 1995, p. 231.

So what can be done? Let's return to John Chrysostom's five preaching principles which we noted in Chapter 2.

1. An excellent knowledge of the Bible

We have already looked at the content of the Christian message. The authority and centrality of the Bible cannot be compromised in preaching that is persuasive and life-changing. When the truth of the Bible is related to human needs, people become interested. Today, however, preachers can no longer take the biblical knowledge of their congregations for granted. Martin Robinson, Director of Mission and Theology at the Bible Society in the UK, said,

> It has taken many decades for the Bible to become a closed book, and we should not imagine that it will be reopened quickly. But if tomorrow is to be filled with genuine hope, then the Bible must be open to all, however long it might take.

The purpose of the Bible is clearly set out in 2 Timothy 3:16:

> All Scripture is God-breathed and is useful for teaching, rebuking, correcting and training in righteousness, so that the man of God may be thoroughly equipped for every good work.

The Bible is powerful in the hands of the Holy Spirit. It produces faith on the part of hearers. It becomes a source of guidance, wisdom, assurance and hope for the future. It encourages, comforts and challenges. It transforms lives and builds people up in their relationship with God and with others. History shows that during times of authentic spiritual revival, the Bible's message changes the lives of many people.

Churches have different approaches to teaching the Bible. Some preachers emphasize verse-by-verse expository preaching; others work steadily through a whole book of the Bible over several Sundays. Some take on topical series; others follow a lectionary designed for the Christian year. Whichever is our preferred method, the important principle is to explain the Bible so that its message becomes understood, relevant and clear.

Roy Clements argues that expository preaching still has a place in a postmodern culture:

> While the style of preaching may well have to be radically revised if it is to communicate effectively in our contemporary world, the expository method must continue to inform the public teaching of any church which wishes to remain securely biblical in its ethos.[2]

Preaching sermons in series and in a consistent style helps to build up the congregation. They know what to expect week by week, and if the message connects with people where they are, then they are more likely to return and encourage others to come with them. There are numerous churches which have demonstrated how this approach can build a congregation almost service by service. Tell people on a Sunday morning what is going to be preached in the evening, or next Sunday morning, and if it is compellingly relevant the congregation will grow. There is clear evidence to prove it.

In the New Testament, Philip explained to the Ethiopian a section of the Old Testament book of Isaiah. The story makes it clear that it is not enough just to read Scripture, for the Ethiopian says, 'How can I understand what I am reading, unless someone explains it to me?' Then comes a statement that challenges every preacher: 'Then Philip began with that very passage of Scripture and told him the

---

[2] Cambridge Papers, Vol. 7, No. 3, September 1998.

good news about Jesus' (Acts 8:35). Philip employed another principle, one that Jesus always used: start where people are, with what they are interested in, then address their need, what is important to them, and the questions they are asking.

In order to 'reopen' the Bible, as Martin Robinson puts it, we need to make it accessible. There is no need to read long, complicated passages in order to preach from them. Read out something simple to understand, but relevant to the day's message, and explain the more complex passage in the course of the sermon. Needless to say, it also helps to read from one of the newer translations of the Bible.

2. A good command of language

As we have seen, Jesus spoke in an attractive manner, for 'the large crowd listened to him with delight' (Mark 12:37). Leith Anderson writes, 'Leaders must be attuned to their culture. It is not enough to know the Bible. We must also know our culture and our people.'[3] He points out that congregations include growing numbers of biblically illiterate people, and suggests using sermon titles and language more familiar to the unchurched. 'Titling a sermon on Luke 18:18–27 "The Guy Who Had Everything and Still Wasn't Satisfied," rather than "The Rich Young Ruler," doesn't make the sermon any less biblical. It makes it more relevant.'[4]

Preachers need to work hard on their language. It is so easy to slip into a sort of 'holy speak'. Three mistakes are commonly made. The first is to speak in theological terms that are familiar to mature believers but not necessarily to younger believers or the unchurched. It is a little like using

---

[3] Leith Anderson, *A Church for the 21st Century*, Bethany House Publishers, 1992, p. 63.
[4] Ibid., p. 205.

complex medical terms to a patient, or aviation terminology to an airline passenger, or film jargon to someone who simply wants to visit the cinema. After John Wesley wrote a sermon, he read it to his maid and then took out any words she did not understand. The problem is that it is far easier for theologically trained clergy to speak in theological terms than it is for them to interpret theology into everyday language. Speak out a sermon to yourself before preaching it to others. What writes well or is well thought out may not necessarily speak well. Sermons are to be heard, not read.

The second mistake is to think we are using everyday language when in reality we are using language from the past. For example, I once heard a preacher describing the storm on Galilee. He was not using any long words, but his vocabulary was out of date. 'When the storm arose . . .' he began, and I wondered how a newsreader would report such an event today. Probably they would say something like, 'When the storm broke . . .' or, 'When the storm hit . . .' Then the preacher said that the disciples 'cried to him in their distress and their cry went unheeded'. Why not just say, 'The disciples were pleading for help.' Put it all in everyday language!

I was once asked by a member of our congregation what the word 'unconditional' meant, after someone had preached a sermon on the unconditional love of God. Someone else asked me what the word 'context' meant. There is a language that is preachy but not necessarily biblical, and that is not the ordinary language of today's culture.

The third mistake is to use only one style of preaching. I know from personal experience that television has changed the rules of communication. It has shortened most people's attention span. It has caused them to have higher expectations of communication. Television bombards people with masses of information, so they are more selective in what they choose to hear. One of Gatwick Airport's terminal duty managers explained why they no longer make flight departure announcements: 'If you have to make a lot of announcements over the PA,' he said, 'passengers go what we call "PA deaf" and simply don't hear them.' Some people in our congregations have become 'sermon deaf' because the style and language are just too familiar. Different sermon content calls for different styles and different language.

If preachers want to get through to their congregations, they need to use language that people understand.

3. A compassionate heart for people

'It is doubtful that there is anything more basic, more Christlike, and therefore more Christian than compassion.'[5] All too often, sermons will beat up rather than lift up. Some hardened evangelical churchgoers do not think they have been to church unless they have been castigated for their lack of commitment. The mood is changing, however. Today's people come to church looking for inspiration, motivation, renewal of spirit and refreshment of mind; they want to be lifted up rather than beaten down.

In most congregations there are emotionally bruised and hurting people. Some have had a tough week and they are wondering how they can face the next. Churches should be places where broken lives can be put back together, where lost people can find purpose and meaning through faith in Christ. In many congregations there are people who are bereaved; people struggling with ill health; people struggling with tense relationships, either at home or in the workplace; people who are facing pressures and tensions of many different kinds, as they try to come to terms with issues of sexuality, finance, parenthood, loneliness, guilt, addictions and all kinds of relational problems.

---

[5] Chuck Swindoll, *Compassion*, Word Books, 1984, p. 39.

As a young minister I remember a businessman telling me there were two ways to make a donkey move forward. One was to offer a carrot, and the other was to give it a sharp smack on the rear with a stick. The implication was clear. Most of my preaching was a kick from behind. The eerie thing was, people seemed to like it! Then I made another discovery. I realized one day that when I preached a practical message of hope, people did not simply listen, they entered into the sermon and began to share it with me. Ephesians 4:29 says, 'Do not let any unwholesome talk come out of your mouths, but only what is helpful for building others up according to their needs.'

Congregations instinctively know when a preacher is speaking from the heart and from personal experience. People identify with preachers when they share something of their own spiritual journey, or their own pressures. Let people know that you understand their struggles. After all, when we read Hebrews 4:15, we feel God is much closer to us:

We do not have a high priest who is unable to sympathise with our weaknesses, but we have one who has been tempted in every way, just as we are – yet was without sin.

G. Campbell Morgan, a famous preacher in the twentieth century, really understood the needs of his generation.

He once listened to an articulate young preacher as he delivered his sermon. A bystander later asked him for his evaluation of the preacher and the sermon. Morgan answered, 'He is a very good preacher and when he has suffered he will be a great preacher.'[6]

Matthew 9:36 reminds us, 'When he [Jesus] saw the crowds, he had compassion on them, because they were

---

[6] Leith Anderson, *A Church for the 21st Century*, p. 203.

harassed and helpless.' Later we are told, 'When Jesus landed and saw a large crowd, he had compassion on them' (14:14). The compassion of Jesus permeates the Gospels. The people sensed it as he moved among them. A preacher who has a compassionate heart for people will know their hurts, pains, fears and hopes. Chuck Swindoll says, 'Others will not care how much we know until they know how much we care.' The Holy Spirit uses compassionate, sensitive preaching to touch the lives of people.

4. An ability to relate theology to everyday life

Remember how Jesus announced his ministry, quoting from Isaiah. He was there to bring 'good news to the poor', 'freedom for the prisoners', 'recovery of sight for the blind', 'to release the oppressed' and 'to proclaim the year of the Lord's favour' (Luke 4:18–19). Jesus later invites people, 'Come to me, all you who are weary and burdened, and I will give you rest' (Matthew 11:28). What an offer! Following Christ means self-denial and cross-bearing on a daily basis, but in the positive context of God's support: 'For whoever wants to save his life will lose it, but whoever loses his life for me and for the gospel will save it' (Mark 8:35).

On the Day of Pentecost, Peter and the disciples preached good news. In answer to the crowd's question, 'What shall we do?' Peter replied,

> Repent and be baptised, every one of you, in the name of Jesus Christ for the forgiveness of your sins. And you will receive the gift of the Holy Spirit. (Acts 2:37–38)

You will not find a better offer anywhere!

Relating the Bible to everyday life is a big challenge for any church. Phillips Brooks defines preaching as 'truth through personality'.[7] He pleads with preachers to open one side of their lives to the truth of God, and the other side to the vast needs of men and women. Then, he says, bring the truth of God to meet the needs of those men and women. Paul describes Christians as 'ministers of reconciliation' trusted with the 'message of reconciliation' (2 Corinthians 5:18–19).

Research by Mark Greene, a former Vice Principal of the London Bible College, suggests that one in two preachers lacked relevance, even though a sermon was considered 'excellent' by congregations.

> The yearning for relevance was not accompanied by any significant level of complaint about the teaching of the Bible. Exegesis is not where people think the problem lies, though it is almost certainly an issue. In fact, most felt that the Bible was being taught, even if many felt it wasn't being applied. Indeed, it was clear that for some it was possible for someone to deliver an 'excellent' sermon that made no connection with their life.
>
> We've been strong on calling for the need to expound the text but less strong on answering people's questions – which is why 50% of evangelicals have never heard a sermon on work. I think it's vital to tackle the Bible book by book, but it's not the only answer. At Pentecost, for example, Peter wasn't preaching on Joel because it was the lectionary reading for the week but because he was being asked a question about grown people who appeared to be slewed out of their minds.[8]

Calvin Miller, a highly respected preacher in the USA, talks about 'marketplace preaching' – reaching people where they are. 'I have discovered,' he says, 'that to grow a church from ten members to 3,500 members, you have to be able to start where the people are.'[9] He calls for preaching that is relational, colloquial and relevant.

---

[7] Phillips Brooks, *Lectures on Preaching*, Allenson, 1902, p. 32.

[8] Mark Greene, *The Three-Eared Preacher*, quoted by *Quadrant*, November 1998, published by Christian Research.

[9] Calvin Miller, interviewed in *Ministry* (SAMA, November 1998), p 12.

I do not believe that preaching to felt needs means we are to preach a gospel of worldly prosperity and success. Preaching that is all success orientated and continually upbeat turns many people away. People are hungry for good news that is earthed in reality. I used to believe it was enough to preach biblical principles and let the congregation work those out for themselves in their everyday lives. That might have been possible even a few decades ago. Today, however, people are looking for help. Application of the message is essential, sometimes to the extent of offering additional help by making people available to talk to when the worship concludes, or by suggesting further books to read or groups to attend. Application means relating theology to everyday life. I believe this is a badly neglected area of proclamation in churches today. We have been strong on exposition, but weak on application.

People are not, of course, concerned only with the present: they are continually looking to the future. What will happen next? How do I prepare? Preaching has a similar role to public broadcasting: both try to prepare people for the future.

> Broadcasting has a role in preparing and training people to come to terms with new ideas and visions: new technologies like computers, e-mail, the Internet; facing the fears and opportunities of new medical practices; questioning new political realities of Europe; new economics; the future needs for employment and unemployment, for wealth or poverty, for education and training.[10]

Part of the role of preaching is to equip people for the future, both in this world and the next.

---

[10] Robert McLeish, Director of Robert McLeish Associates Management and Media Training Consultancy.

More than ever before, the need for preaching to be practical and relevant, as well as biblical, is paramount. We
should speak to the needs of the congregation in such a
way that our preaching makes an ongoing difference to
people's lives. American preachers tend to be better at this
than their British counterparts, although they sometimes
go too far and fill the entire sermon with much application
but very little content. The British, on the other hand, tend
to spend too much time on history and doctrine. I wish I
had understood years ago what I have come to know the
hard way – how to apply the message. Rick Warren puts
this need in a nutshell when he says, 'Tell them why; show
them how.'

Much has been written about the move from deductive to
inductive preaching. Fred Craddock, a professor of preaching and New Testament, was asked why he championed
inductive biblical preaching so much. He explained that he
was 'giving the listeners room to arrive at conclusions rather
than concluding and then preaching on it'.

Inductive preaching is not to be confused with lack of
application. Inductive preaching, or reasoning, starts with a
need or experience, moves on to the general truth and then
applies it in a way that enables the listeners to make the
sermon theirs and draw their own conclusions. For example,
an inductive sermon may start with people's need for love,
provide stories and examples of God's love in people's lives,
state that God demonstrated love when he sent Jesus, and so
reach the conclusion that 'God is love'. Deductive preaching
starts with a general truth, explains it, and moves on to particular applications. This kind of sermon often has an introduction, three key points, and a clear conclusion calling for a
decision. Deductive preaching is rather like a film which
starts out by telling you what the film is about and what the
end of the story is. Inductive preaching is more like a film that
keeps you guessing and allows you to work out the plot for

yourself. Deductive preaching focuses more on telling the congregation what to do, using parental words such as 'ought', 'should', and 'must'. Inductive preaching explains the issues, presents the alternatives and then seeks to persuade, but leaves the decision up to the listeners. It does not start with a proposition, but unfolds slowly, allowing the listeners to participate and plot a journey of discovery for themselves. This is not to say that one style is right and the other wrong. They are just different, and one style might be more appropriate for a specific occasion or congregation than the other. Many sermons are, in fact, a combination of both.

The Bible, and the New Testament in particular, was written to help people with specific problems and needs. Likewise, our preaching should always be concerned with addressing the real needs in people's lives, the issues and current concerns that people share.

Teaching Bible knowledge alone can achieve little. Although it may be truth, at that moment it may be irrelevant truth to the listeners. One of the mistakes often made is to overload listeners with information about the biblical text. My former Associate Pastor, Steve Chalke, now a broadcaster and Founding Director of Oasis Trust, describes a common problem:

> The previous week had been difficult. As I sat in my pew that Sunday morning, I was at my wits' end. But rather than providing the help that I so desperately needed, the sermon – which dealt in some depth with the three Hebrew words for 'worship' used in one of the Psalms – only multiplied my frustration and despair. I left the building after the service, praying, with all the sarcasm I could muster, 'Well thanks God! I'm really struggling to be a sensitive husband, wise father, good boss, loyal friend and responsible member of society. I can't say I've had much help in any of these areas, but at least I now have a better grasp of some Hebrew words for worship!'

Steve goes on to say that positive preaching addresses human needs and issues with a clear, practical spirituality that ordinary people can understand, relate to and benefit from. 'So many sermons on so many Sundays in so many churches are theologically sound, exegetically precise and practically irrelevant.' Preaching needs to move *from* people's concerns and situations *to* the Bible. Doing it the other way round increases the danger of being abstract. As 1 Corinthians 14:3 reminds us, 'Everyone who prophesies speaks to men for their strengthening, encouragement and comfort.'

5. A passionate enthusiasm when preaching

Preaching should be done with energy, passion and enthusiasm. The potential effect of good content can be lost if the delivery is dull and lifeless. People are looking at the messenger as well as listening to the message. Is the messenger committed to his or her message? Does it come from the heart? Phillips Brooks writes,

> Truth must come through the person, not merely over his lips, not merely into his understanding and out through his pen. It must come through his character, his affections, his whole intellectual and moral being.[11]

Do not try to be someone you are not. Be true to yourself and to your own convictions, but also be true to your text.

How often we have heard sections from the Bible which describe joy and hope read in a manner that conveys the opposite. Reading the Bible in a dull manner is being less than responsible to the congregation. The same principles apply to public praying, and to the sermon. Phillips Brooks

---

[11] Phillips Brooks *Lectures on Preaching*, p. 8.

makes the point that the sermon is a 'message' of which we are 'witnesses', as Peter says to his opponents.

> In these two words together, I think, we have the fundamental conception of the matter of all Christian preaching. It is to be a message given to us for transmission, but yet a message which we cannot transmit until it has entered into our own experience, and we can give our testimony of its spiritual power. The minister who keeps the word 'message' always written before him, as he prepares his sermon in the study, or utters from the pulpit, is saved from the tendency to wanton and wild speculation, and from the mere passion of originality. He who never forgets that word 'witness', is saved from the unreality of repeating by rote mere forms of statement which he has learned as orthodox, but never realised as true.[12]

If the messenger is gripped and excited by his message, then the congregation is more likely to be gripped and motivated by the message as well. We are reminded in 2 Corinthians 5:19–20 that God

> has committed to us the message of reconciliation. We are therefore Christ's ambassadors, as though God were making his appeal through us. We implore you on Christ's behalf: Be reconciled to God.

Preaching with a passionate enthusiasm does not mean we have to shout. With good sound equipment in many buildings, preaching has developed into a more conversational style, but enthusiasm, passion and conviction still need to be present. In Acts 2:40, Peter 'pleaded' with his hearers.

Preaching with passionate enthusiasm is not be confused with preaching only what people want to hear. It is not a compromise of the gospel. It is a communication of the gospel in terms of what it is – 'good news'. When Jesus

---

[12] Ibid., pp. 14–15.

preached and taught, he dealt with all kinds of human needs and conditions. He talked about money, food, clothing, forgiveness, fear, human relationships, and about how to overcome all kinds of hang-ups and habits such as lying, cheating, destructive use of sex, prejudice, anger, hatred and murder. As the *News of the World* used to advertise itself, 'All human life is here.'

The primary goal of preaching is to change lives. The application of the sermon is to call for some form of commitment. Usually that is a process rather than a moment in time. Being well prepared for preaching in the twenty-first century will mean far more than having three points and a poem to offer. Sometimes there is too much theory and too little practicality. We need a mix of theory and practice. This means that old sermons from previous years just won't do. I am constantly changing in my style and presentation. It is important to stay fresh, positive, and relevant to today's needs.

The postmodern age

Postmodernism, which developed first among academics and artists, has spread throughout our culture. At its most basic level, postmodernism means the passing of the 'modern times' where confidence in science and technology was high. Modernity was supposed to provide an end to all our conflicts and problems. By the end of the twentieth century, however, despite advances in science, medicine and technology, it had finally dawned on us that none of these accomplishments could save us from the problems and evils that plague us. So modernity has been rejected, and a 'postmodern' age has come.

Postmodernism is not so much a movement as a mood. It is a mood which sets itself apart from the certainties of the modern age. It conveys the idea that truth is now more elusive than ever. The new truth is constantly changing with today's definitions of relevance and social acceptance. This, of course, makes other faiths and lifestyles more acceptable than in the past. In particular, younger generations may be more open to hearing about Jesus Christ, but they may be proud that they tolerate other faiths as well. They might reject the church, but not necessarily God. All of this affects the way we communicate the Christian faith. We need to understand something of the mood and thinking of post-modern men and women.

> Values in post-modern society have gone relative. We're told it's the end of a meta-narrative, the big explanation, the big Utopia. Instead you make up and write your own agenda.[13]

It is imperative that the church understands the world in which it serves. A growing church that is communicating effectively will not be a church locked in a time warp of mid-twentieth-century ways of thinking. Nevertheless, we should not become obsessed with postmodernism. Some churches, in their desire to communicate to the surrounding culture, have become like that culture. The church is called to be a counterculture.

> Modern culture is revolt against the truth, and postmodernism is but the latest form of this revolt. Ministry in these strange times calls for undiluted conviction and faithful apologetics. The temptations to compromise are great, and the opposition which comes to anyone who would claim to preach absolute and eternal truth is severe. But this is the task of the believing church.[14]

---

[13] Elaine Storkey, speaking at *Women in Mission* 1997, quoted in *Woman Alive* magazine.
[14] Albert Mohler, *The Tie*, Vol. 65, No. 2, Southern Seminary, Kentucky, Spring 1997.

How can the church today be an effective evangelist in a postmodern world? Our congregations and communities may not understand fully what is behind the moods and fancies of our day, but they do know that we live in a very different spiritual and moral environment from previous generations, and that only a true spiritual revival will cut through it all. In the meantime, we can help our congregations to understand the world in which they minister, and to understand why people think and behave in the way they do. Coming to grips with the culture may be part of the preparation for true revival.

> The West appears to have said its definitive farewell to a Christian culture. Our secular colleagues are happy to recognise the debt our civilisation owes to the Christian faith to the extent that the faith, having been absorbed by culture itself, has become simply another cultural artifact. Christianity has become a historical factor subservient to a secular culture rather than functioning as the creative power it once was.[15]

Whatever may have been the case in the past, in today's culture the whole church needs to be involved in the process of evangelism. It cannot be left to mass crusades and special events of outreach. Evangelism is a process, and the whole church, day by day, week by week, year by year, is to be involved. This is the purpose of the whole church, not just one group within it.

> As we approach the 21st Century, our obedience must be no less than that of the first-century church. We must proclaim and teach boldly the Word of God. We must be willing to take the gospel message into a culture that insists we keep our religion to ourselves. And we must let Scripture determine our methods

---

[15] Louis Dupre, Yale Professor, quoted in *Christian Century*, July 1997, p. 654.

and message rather than adjusting to the daily whims of culture.[16]

Positive preaching does not win a positive response from everyone. When Jesus stood up in the synagogue in Nazareth and announced his mission, he made positive statements – and was promptly almost killed. The gospel is essentially good news, but not everyone recognizes it as such. That is no reason for not making it known, however! Even repentance can be preached in a positive way: turning from darkness to light, from blindness to sight, from lost to found, from death to life. Some preachers seem to emphasize what the Bible is against rather than the hope it embraces. Joel Edwards, General Director of the UK Evangelical Alliance, has said, 'Our most important task is not to become experts in describing the darkness.'

As Religious Advisor to one of the ITV companies and part of the *Morning Worship* team for the ITV Network, as well as the *Sunday Morning* programme, one of my frequent responsibilities has been to read sermon manuscripts submitted by preachers for television. It is amazing to me how many sermons begin (and in some cases continue) negatively. The preachers have approximately eight minutes of television time in which to reach the largest congregation any minister is likely to have in the whole of their lifetime, yet often their message is phrased in off-putting, negative terms.

Preaching a positive message is not the same as compromising the message. Jesus preached repentance in a positive way, but never compromised the truth. Mark tells us at the beginning of his Gospel, 'Jesus went into Galilee proclaiming the good news of God. "The time has come," he said. "The kingdom of God is near. Repent and believe the good news"' (Mark 1:14–15).

---

[16] Thom S. Rainer, *The Tie*, Spring 1997, p. 12.

Ravi Zacharias at Amsterdam 2000 said,

> We have often heard it said that a picture is better than a thousand words. I would like to suggest that a well-chosen word is better than a thousand pictures.

More than ever in this postmodern age, people need to hear the gospel preached positively, vividly and with commitment.

5

Practical Principles for the Twenty-first Century

'How do you like my sermon, Mr Canning?' a clergyman once asked the ninetheenth-century Prime Minister. 'You were brief,' replied the PM. 'Yes,' said the preacher, 'you know I avoid being tedious.' 'But you were tedious,' said Mr Canning.

After a long and rambling oration Winston Churchill said, 'I am sorry to have made such a long speech, but I did not have time to write a shorter one.'

The late Dr Reinhold Niebuhr decided to write out his theological position, stating exactly where he stood philosophically – his credo. Being the profound thinker he was (and a bit verbose), it took him many sheets of paper to express himself. Upon completion of his masterwork, he realised it was in need of being read and evaluated by a mind much more practical than his own. He bundled up the material and sent it to a minister whom he knew had a practical mind and a pastoral 'heart'.

With great pains the clergyman sweated through this ream of paper, trying desperately to grasp the meaning. When he finally finished, he worked up the nerve to write a brief yet absolutely candid note in reply. It read:

My dear Dr Niebuhr

I understand every word you have written, but I do not understand one sentence.[1]

In spite of the fact that many clergy make teaching and preaching their primary task, many of us still fail to communicate. A theological college tutor who had been a local minister for at least 15 years found himself sitting in the pew more often than he used to. He remarked to me, 'It scares me to think what I was doing in the pulpit week after week. I now realize that when I sit in the pew after a hard week, I need something to lift me up, to inspire and motivate me. What I mostly get is a scolding for not being more committed.' Perhaps many of us as preachers do not spend enough time sitting where our people sit. This is possibly the main reason why we miss the mark so often in our preaching.

Preaching for encouragement and pastoral care

One of the great purposes of preaching is to put heart into downhearted, discouraged people. Intentionally preaching to lift people up is a ministry of encouragement. Without it, a congregation will begin to feel that their preacher does not really understand them, or even care for them, and that they are taken for granted.

The apostle Paul was intentional about lifting people up. He does it repeatedly in his letters. He gives thanks for the people. He lets them know he has great affection for them. He inspires and motivates them. He tells them not to tire of doing good, for they will reap a great harvest if they keep going. The ministry of encouragement is a valued pastoral function, and part of that comes through the pastoral care shown in preaching.

---

[1] Chuck Swindoll, *Compassion*, Word Books, 1984, pp. 20–21.

Many people are looking for meaning and significance in their lives, not more information. We need to ask ourselves, 'Does the sermon each week lift people up or beat people up?' In addition, many preachers spend too much time on introductions and exegesis and too little time on application. Sometimes as much as 90 per cent of the sermon can be interpretation or background study, and only the last few minutes are devoted to application. Week by week, among our listeners will be discouraged men and women, people struggling with relationships, ill health, bereavement, unemployment, or uncertainty about the future. We therefore need to ask, 'How can I best help this person today to find strength and inspiration?' The answer will inevitably cause us to pay more attention to applying the message rather than just interpreting it.

Preaching for a purpose

This is the way Jesus preached. He did not just give out information. He called for action – and there were many different kinds of action, depending on who he was speaking to. So often, preaching for commitment is limited to a challenge to accept Christ, come forward for prayer, or join the church. It can be so much more than that. People are hungry for practical steps to take on their spiritual journey, and long to be shown what those steps are and how they can be taken. They want to know how they can apply what they have heard.

Preaching for a purpose may involve talking about how to handle peer pressure, how to resist the temptation to compromise, how to build better relationships, how to develop a closer relationship with God, how to be part of a small group in the church, how to cope with suffering, how to help and support others with the same comfort we ourselves have received. Holistic evangelism will address the daily problems of people's lives, their involvement with the intimate experiences of friends and neighbours, and real-life challenges within the community. Matters relating to personal finances, marriage and family, sex, study, physical fitness, employment, addictions and human rights can all be addressed. Whatever the need, it cries out for transformation, healing, liberation and salvation, with the gospel message overarching and undergirding everything that is proclaimed.

Preaching for a purpose may also involve a strong encouragement to take certain spiritual steps in a prescribed period of time, perhaps a month, three months, or a year. People could be urged, for example, to study a book of the Bible once a quarter, to read one good theological book each year, or to go on a short-term mission trip to another culture. When this kind of action is called for, the message must be appropriately backed up: by making books, tapes and CDs available, or providing information about people to see or groups to join. If possible, such support should be available immediately after the worship service is over. People will be interested. They will want to respond. Never underestimate the effect of preaching with a purpose.

Preaching for changed lives

The result of preaching should be changed lives, not just better informed people. Obviously change is based on information, but all too often a 'teaching' sermon is high on information and low on application. We need to reverse that ratio. We can still teach: in fact, the best teaching sermons are those which call for change by informing people's minds, engaging their emotions and challenging their will. I have discovered that application-based sermons which explain the Bible are frequently recognized by mature Christians as 'good teaching'. When members of our congregations feel challenged to change, they understand that as being taught and spiritually fed. Instead of leaving church saying, 'That was a good sermon' (rather like saying, 'That is a fine painting,' i.e., commenting on the sermon as an art form rather than a rallying cry), they feel they have truly been taught. They have not only received interpretation of Scripture or good exegesis, but they have heard the challenge to change as well.

Of course, it is not the preacher who brings about the ultimate change in belief and behaviour as a result of a preached message; it is God who changes people's minds. Our task is to bring people into contact with God's revelation of himself through Christ and through his written word. The Holy Spirit, working through both the preacher and the listener, brings about the change. Repentance is where people go 'from darkness to light, from guilt to forgiveness, from no hope to hope, from no purpose to purpose',[2] from living for themselves to living for Christ. It is the ultimate paradigm shift, changing minds at the deepest level of beliefs and values. This is the work of God. We are simply the means of communication that he chooses to use.

It is vital to try to sense where the congregation is at any particular time, where they need to go and what they should do. The story is told of a student who preached before the great Victorian 'Prince of Preachers', Charles Haddon Spurgeon. At the end of the sermon, the student said to Spurgeon, 'Will it do, sir, will it do?' To which Spurgeon replied, 'Do what?' Sadly, the same could be said of many sermons today. Always aim for a specific action. James 1:22 says, 'Do not merely listen to the word, and so deceive yourselves. Do what it says.'

The needs of the congregation are best discovered through conversations with individuals. Without interaction

---

[2] Rick Warren in an interview for the magazine *Preaching*, Preaching Resources Inc., September 2001.

with the people in our churches and our communities, we will never know their needs. We must develop a pastoral heart. We should constantly be asking what people are thinking about. What are the issues that concern them at the moment? All effective communicators start with where people are. Effective teachers start with the student rather than the curriculum. The story of Philip in Acts 8:30–35 is a prime example of starting with where people are. Paul did the same when he was preaching in Athens (Acts 17:22–34). Mark Greene says,

> 54% of Jesus' reported teaching ministry arose out of issues posed by others. He answered people's questions – spoken and unspoken. Peter's agenda in Acts 2 was not set by a lectionary . . . but by people's questions about the extraordinary behaviour they had just seen.[3]

It is strange that the proclamation of the Christian gospel – the sermon, if you like – has such a capacity to cause boredom, and yet it also has an enormous capacity to provide excitement and motivation. Why do we allow the former to rob us of the latter? Poor preaching is killing hundreds of churches. Effective, relevant preaching is the ultimate tool for church health.

Preaching in series

Structuring your preaching in organized series can create helpful continuity and momentum. It gets away from the idea of 'going to church' being a one-off occasion that makes people feel they have done their bit. Preaching a series of messages on a theme can create expectation, a

---

[3] Mark Greene, *Supporting Christians at Work*, 'How-to Guide' Vol. 2, No. 6, Administry, 2001, pp. 24–25, 72.

sense of journeying somewhere, and a sense of purpose that comes across even to visitors.

In my own church, to emphasize this sense of journey, we print out all the sermons in a series and provide audio tapes. We might give out up to 30 or 40 tapes on a Sunday, but the transcripts are much more popular and we often hand out 300 to 400 of these. People do not always have time to listen to tapes, and if a particular part of a message has been especially relevant to them, they can find it more quickly in a transcript than on a tape. We encourage people to pick up the transcripts of sermons they have missed, so they do not miss the overall message we believe God has for us at a particular season of the year. Even if regular members of the congregation are away – and rarely do people these days attend enough to hear all the sermons in a longer series – they do not miss out. We also encourage visitors who may have heard only one sermon to order the transcripts of the whole series. During one summer, while we were preaching through the Ten Commandments, many visitors did just that. Our church office sent out over 300 complete sets of that sermon series to people in many different parts of the country.

Producing transcripts requires discipline and planning. Either someone will take the sermon down in shorthand, or will transcribe an audio tape, or the preacher will produce a full manuscript. I personally believe that every preacher can benefit from the discipline of writing out a full script every now and again. What writes well does not necessarily speak well, however, and it can also be a good practice to take only partial notes into the pulpit. Use key words and headings to remind you of the various sections of your message. Some important points or statements, or key quotations, can be written out in full to make sure you do not miss them out. Writing out in full your key points can also help to increase your confidence and sharpen up your communication skills. Always ask yourself: 'Can I say this better? Can I say it more clearly? Can I say it more simply?'

There are a few people who can preach effectively from a full script, but you would never know that they have all the words written down in front of them. They are not merely good readers: usually they have rehearsed the delivery of their message carefully, marking the script in key places. The Scottish preacher Peter Marshall typed all his sentences out with certain indentations so that they formed a shape on the page, which helped him to know exactly where he was in his message. Here is an example from one of his sermons:

> Many of you – like Nicodemus – have come close to Jesus.
>   Perhaps you too have felt the nudge
>   the uneasy feeling in your own conscience
>   the tugging at the heart
>   the resolves that spring up every now and then
>   the longing to do something special
>   to *be* someone . . .
> Could not that be Christ calling you?
> And you have waited.
>   You waited to respond
>   But you waited.
> Remember that He will not force Himself upon you.
> He will not assault you, or intrude where He is not wanted.
> Christ will let you go through the years, using no restraint or
> compulsion beyond the appeal that He is constantly making –
>   To your better nature
>   To your loyalty
>   Your gratitude
>   Your recognition of the imperishables,
> The hunger of your own young heart.[4]

---

[4] Peter Marshall, *John Doe, Disciple*, edited by Catherine Marshall, McGraw-Hill, 1963, p. 136.

Some preachers can 'hoover' up whole paragraphs at a time, speak the words looking at their audience, then look back to their notes and 'hoover' up some more. You can tell that they are not just reading their script, because they are communicating their message with such vitality and energy. They are interacting with their listeners.

Many communicators practise delivering their message. There is nothing wrong with that at all. People who make business presentations, speeches or sales pitches, and many television and radio presenters, often rehearse very carefully. Why not rehearse the message you are planning to share with your congregation? It is, after all, potentially of life-changing importance.

One advantage of having two identical worship services in our church on a Sunday is that the same sermon is preached twice. Those of us on the preaching team all agree that the second time is usually the best. Not only are we more famil-iar with our material and therefore less likely to rely so much on our notes, but we have probably used a red pencil, sharp-ened up our communication skills and learned from our initial mistakes. The difference between a good sermon and a more effective one is often the delivery not the content.

Good preaching can create expectation and a sense of purpose that can be felt even before the worship service begins. Announcing a particular series ahead of time enables members of the congregation to come prepared and to invite non-churchgoing friends to come with them. Congregations will do this if they know what subjects or themes are coming up. If they do not know what the sermon is going to be about, or whether it is going to be relevant, they will not have the confidence to bring their friends. On the contrary, they are often very reluctant to invite their friends and neighbours to church, worried that the sermon may be irrelevant or boring, or, worse, that they will be hit with an appeal for money.

Preaching in series is a good practice, but it is best to avoid long series. A series on the Ten Commandments is obviously going to involve ten sermons – people expect that – but normally an effective series will last for no more than six weeks. If you do have a twelve-week series planned, break it up into two six-week series. Have a break. Invite a visiting speaker. Have a different type of worship service. That way you will keep the expectation and interest alive.

Preaching with understanding

I always say to myself and my colleagues, 'Say what the sermon is about in one sentence.' Or ask the question, 'What is it you are wanting people to do?' and answer that question in a single sentence. Make that sentence the title of your message, not only for the benefit of the congregation, but to focus your own mind. If you are not sure what you are saying, your congregation will not know either.

I once heard a frustrated religious affairs correspondent from a national daily newspaper say, 'The problem of the church is: They don't know what to say and they don't know how to say it.' Compare that once again with Jesus' words recorded in John 12:49: 'For I did not speak of my own accord, but the Father who sent me commanded me what to say and how to say it.'

Know your congregation, the people with whom you are trying to communicate. The best communication happens when the preacher and congregation know each other. The preacher is then an inspirer and interpreter of the situations in which he or she and the listeners find themselves. It is often the case that a visiting preacher, who is worth travelling miles to hear in his or her own church, is not nearly as effective away from that home congregation. Pastors, vicars, priests, deacons, lay preachers and lay readers will all be more effective communicators if they stay in constant touch with the concerns and needs of their congregations.

On a very practical note, I have helped myself in my teaching and preaching preparation by asking the following questions.

1. To whom will I be preaching?

Who will be in the congregation? What are the issues they are facing? What is their local culture? What are the needs of their local community? What kind of background do they have? I love what Paul says in 1 Corinthians 9:19–23:

> Though I am free and belong to no man, I make myself a slave to everyone, to win as many as possible. To the Jews I became like a Jew, to win the Jews. To those under the law I became like one under the law (though I myself am not under the law), so as to win those under the law. To those not having the law I became like one not having the law (though I am not free from God's law but am under Christ's law), so as to win those not having the law. To the weak I became weak, to win the weak. I have become all things to all men so that by all possible means I might save some. I do all this for the sake of the gospel, that I may share in its blessings.

I like this even better in the Living Bible paraphrase:

> When I am with those whose consciences bother them easily, I don't act as though I know it all and don't say they are foolish; the result is that they are willing to let me help them. Yes, whatever a person is like, I try to find common ground with [them] so that [they] will let me tell [them] about Christ and let Christ save [them]. I do this to get the Gospel to them and also for blessing I myself receive when I see them come to Christ.

2. Will the message capture the attention of people?

Will my message deal with the real questions and hurts of the people in front of me and provide me with an opportunity to teach the truth? Will I really engage their minds, hearts and wills?

3. Is the sermon title clear to both preacher and congregation?

Does the title say in a sentence what the sermon is about? Some sermon titles say very little about the message. Here are some examples: 'In All Things Enriched by Him', 'Either He Is or He Isn't', 'Concerning the Collection', 'A River in the Wilderness', 'Where Is the Far Country?' Do you think those titles would attract anyone to your church? The last one would probably be understood by Christians as having something to do with the parable of the Prodigal Son. Then again, it might not. I am just guessing, and no one else would be any the wiser either!

Examples of more positive sermon titles that we have collected or used include: 'The Strength of Gentleness', 'Facing the Future Without Fear', 'What Would Jesus Do With My Money?' and 'Showing Care in a Careless World'.

4. Is the message good news?

I have already made a plea for positive preaching and warned against the perils of negative preaching. A sermon may not be negative in itself, but the way it is presented can have a negative effect. I have seen this happen many times with scripts prepared by preachers for television broadcasts. Rick Warren says,

> Years ago I preached a message on the ways we miss God's blessing due to our sinfulness. I titled the sermon 'Why No Revival?' Later I revised the title to 'What Brings Revival?' It was the same message, only restated in positive terms. I believe God blessed the latter message in a far greater way.

Preaching has a vital part to play in teaching and communicating the gospel, but it is not the only way. In the next couple of chapters we will move on to look at how our actions can speak even louder than our words.

PART 3

The Living Word

6

Lifestyle and Communication

A book on Christian communication would not be complete without at least a brief chapter on the importance of lifestyle. What we are will always speak louder than what we say. In today's world, people look hard at the messenger as well as the message, and they quickly detect a phoney.

Lifestyle communication of the Christian gospel is particularly important in the workplace. Living out the gospel is a powerful form of communicating it. When, over a period of time, people see someone consistently living out Christian principles and values, they begin to take notice. Integrity might not always be popular, but it always gets noticed. 'So whether you eat or drink or whatever you do, do it all for the glory of God' (1 Corinthians 10:31). Christians need to understand that their work matters to God.

Life messages

Every person's life has a message. This is what they are remembered for. Some people will be remembered for qualities such as generosity, encouragement and strong faith. Some will be known for their honesty, some for their love, some for their gentleness. Other people, however, will be remembered for their meanness, or their harshness, or their unkindness. What life messages come to mind when you think of Mother Teresa, Martin Luther King, Mahatma Gandhi or Adolf Hitler? What message do you want to communicate with your own life?

Alfred Nobel, the Swedish chemist and engineer, saw his obituary printed in a newspaper by mistake. When he read it, he realized that he was going to be remembered for the manufacture of explosives. He invented dynamite in 1867, gelignite in 1875 and ballistite, a smokeless gunpowder, in 1887. He was shocked by what he read and decided that he wanted to be remembered for something more constructive. He arranged to leave his large fortune in trust for the endowment of five Nobel prizes, the most famous of which is the peace prize, awarded by a committee of the Norwegian parliament.

In the nineteenth century, a newspaper in Boston, USA, printed this comment: 'It was a dull, rainy day, when things looked dark and lowering, but Phillips Brooks (Bishop of Boston) came down through Newspaper Row and all was bright.' A truly Christlike attitude is a potent way of communicating the faith.

People are quick to recognize hypocrisy and pretence. They can also recognize authenticity. After one particular BBC broadcast service, a Senior Producer for the BBC made the comment, 'I've been listening again to the sermon. It's excellent. One of the best in a long time. He seems a fine person – everything he said was credible and impressive, because of the tone of the man.'

People can tell the difference between a genuine Christian and someone who is only paying lip service to the faith. Jesus not only communicated the teaching in the Sermon on the Mount with words, but he lived it out in its entirety. He was the one who said we should act on his words. In Matthew 7:24 he says, 'Therefore everyone who hears these words of mine and puts them into practice is like a wise man who built his house on the rock.' Then in verse 26 we have the contrast, 'But everyone who hears these words of mine and does not put them into practice is like a foolish man who built his house on sand.' Those words apply to us not only before we are believers, but also after we have made a commitment of faith. Even as Christians we can ignore the commands of Christ – and it will be noticed, at home, at work, in the community and in the church.

Lee Strobel used to be a reporter for the *Chicago Tribune* before he became a Christian and later joined the staff of the well-known Willow Creek Church. He says,

> When I walked into church as a sceptical unbeliever, my 'hypocrisy antenna' was scanning the place for signs that people were just playing church. In fact, I was aggressively on the lookout for phoniness, opportunism, or deception, because I felt that if I could find an excuse for rejecting the church on grounds of hypocrisy, I could feel free to reject Christianity as well.[1]

Bill Hybels, Pastor of Willow Creek, says that Lee was won to faith by finding a church filled with people 'who were sincere in their efforts to figure out what it means to please and follow Christ in their daily lives'.

I often reflect on what made the biblical character of Zacchaeus have such a change of heart. He was obviously interested in Jesus. He wanted to see for himself who this man was. What he did not expect was that Jesus would invite himself to his home. There Zacchaeus made an extraordinary confession, indicating his intention to undergo a radical change of character.

---

[1] Bill Hybels, *Becoming a Contagious Christian*, Zondervan, 1994, pp. 68–69.

But Zacchaeus stood up and said to the Lord, 'Look, Lord! Here and now I give half of my possessions to the poor, and if I have cheated anybody out of anything, I will pay back four times the amount.' (Luke 19:8)

What was it that made such an impact on Zacchaeus? Was it the words of Jesus? They were necessary, certainly, but it was who Jesus was that made the difference. I can imagine him saying, 'Here is the first religious person I have met who seems to understand where I am coming from!' The accepting, transparent character of Jesus caused Zacchaeus to think hard about his own character and lifestyle.

Jesus called his followers to be 'salt' and 'light' in the world. Living a life of true New Testament standards of behaviour communicates immediately and powerfully. 'Your attitude should be the same as that of Christ Jesus' (Philippians 2:5). The servant attitude of Jesus is to be the servant attitude of every believer who follows him.

Through the eyes of Christ

Years ago I remember learning that no one I met was a total stranger. As a Christian, there were always at least two things I knew about the other person. First, they were someone whom God loved enough to want to create after his own image. Second, they were someone whom Christ loved enough to want to die for. It was like looking at everyone through new eyes; like seeing everyone through the lenses of a properly adjusted pair of spectacles. Have you got your glasses on? Are you seeing people through the eyes of Christ?

There are probably many people we meet in the course of a day or week whom we just do not see as persons, let alone through the eyes of Jesus. Think about the people who serve you in supermarkets, petrol stations, banks and other places where you routinely go. When you look such people in the eye, call them by their name (if they have a name tag) and take an interest in them as persons, the reactions are sometimes surprising. Some will take no notice and ignore you, but that is not an excuse to stop your efforts. Why should we let others control our attitude? Others will suddenly spring to life, as if to say, 'Someone has actually realized I exist!'

Regarding people through the eyes of Christ can open up all kinds of future opportunities for Christian ministry and witness. Whenever I start consciously to walk through a whole day seeing people in this way, men and women I would otherwise overlook seem suddenly to become noticeable individuals. With a quick question, a listening ear, or an interested look, we can create a '30-second island' of caring in someone's otherwise impersonal day.

Changing our focus from the distant horizon of tomorrow or next week to the immediate events of the moment, and seeing them as important events, opens up rich opportunities for deeper avenues of communication, perhaps at a later time. To act out of love, whether we feel like it or not, is the essence of one-to-one Christian communication. Connecting with people is our priority, and we must do it not only by what we say, but also by who we are. As 2 Corinthians 5:18–19 reminds us, we are 'ministers' as well as 'messengers' of reconciliation.

> All this is from God, who reconciled us to himself through Christ and gave us the ministry of reconciliation: that God was reconciling the world to himself in Christ, not counting men's sins against them. And he has committed to us the message of reconciliation.

The life of the church

The same principles of lifestyle also apply to the church as a whole. The local church will be recognized for its authenticity, or otherwise. The way it relates to the community, whether that is an inner-city, rural or suburban culture, is all important. Without being patronizing, we need to show we have a genuine love and concern for the community and the people who belong to it. As has already been said, 'People will not care how much we know, until they know how much we care.' Like Jesus, it is important that we care with no strings attached. What gladdened and surprised the hearts of many people who experienced Christ's ministry, particularly those among the poor and the struggling in society, was that here was someone who genuinely loved them, with no angles. He just wanted the best for them. He was moved with compassion when he saw them harassed and helpless, as sheep without a shepherd.

We must show that the local church is an inclusive community. No one is second rate or unimportant. The church has the capacity to show what society can be like in terms of people having a sense of belonging, working together, pooling resources, recognizing differences without letting those differences divide them, and learning how to handle conflict without the community becoming dysfunctional.

Sometimes I think that larger churches have a greater sense of unity than some smaller ones. In smaller churches we get to know each other very well and can therefore see each other's faults and weaknesses. The challenge to work together is therefore greater. Sadly, there are far too many dysfunctional churches. There are too many churches who communicate exclusiveness. There are too many churches where people love each other, but do not love the community, the stranger or the visitor. One of the ways to change this is to focus on the community and not on ourselves. That seems so obvious. Why then does it not happen more often?

Some churches need to change their own culture and become more accepting. Growing an accepting, caring and loving atmosphere within a church may take time, however, particularly if there has been a history of broken relationships and poorly handled conflict situations. Nevertheless, there is nothing quite so exciting as watching people grow in their unity, their sense of belonging, and their genuine love and concern. The apostle Paul writes in 2 Thessalonians 1:3, 'We ought always to thank God for you, brothers, and rightly so, because your faith is growing more and more, and the love every one of you has for each other is increasing.'

What a great character reference for any church. As a Christian minister, this has always been my aim for every church I have pastored, and it is thrilling to see it happen. When it happens, the church grows. This kind of love attracts people. You cannot keep this inside the four walls of a church building. The word gets out, and the church gets a reputation for love and care. It communicates. Its message cannot be kept quiet. This is the secret of church health and growth: genuine love in action gets the attention of any community. We have to be intentional, however, and we have to find ways to let it happen.

In order to communicate and build bridges with the community around us, we must discover its needs: loneliness, unemployment, addictions, broken relationships, single-parenting, poverty; or perhaps it is too much materialism, with all the anxiety that can come with it. In the parable of the sower, Jesus described the seed that fell among thorns as representing those who 'hear the word; but the worries of this life, the deceitfulness of wealth and the desires for other things come in and choke the word, making it unfruitful' (Mark 4:19). These are needy people too. Jesus said in Mark 10:23, 'How hard it is for the rich to enter the kingdom of God!'

Perhaps the greatest challenge facing the church in the twenty-first century is to learn how to give a cup of cold water in the name of Jesus (Matthew 10:42). There are two distinct aspects to this challenge: the serving, helping element, and the meaning and motivation element. Often the church has focused on only one aspect of this ministry.

Some Christians are tempted to turn their backs on all that is represented by 'the name of Jesus' and concentrate solely on humanitarianism. The name of Jesus must somehow be involved as well, however, to make possible the discovery of meaning, motivation and the freedom to give one's life in service. Others are tempted to ignore the humanitarian aspect, 'the cup of cold water', and focus totally on proclaiming the name of Jesus. In order to communicate the character of God, his love, grace and mercy, we need to keep these two elements in balance. Our humanitarian idealism is ultimately rooted in our relationship with God. Learning to give a cup of cold water in the name of Jesus is one of the greatest challenges facing Christians.

Reaching out

Our church has a number of support groups. Our intention is that people will find in these groups the support, encouragement, motivation and accountability that we all need. There is a support group for those recently bereaved or struggling with a long-term sense of loss. There are support groups for parents of young children, and parenting courses. There are groups for those with learning difficulties and those who are physically disabled. We have qualified counsellors for those who are struggling with relationships and other challenges and difficulties. There are also work teams involved in providing practical help such as shopping, gardening and transport to and from hospitals. Some teams go to other nearby towns to help with soup runs and care for the homeless.

We also arrange events that are appealing to all ages in the community. Some are regular weekly events such as a coffee shop, a parents and toddlers group, an aerobic evening, as well as the weekend worship services. Some events are one-off, related to our sports ministry, or special events to which our own people can safely invite their friends, such as a visit from a well-known celebrity with a story to tell, or music events. These occasions gradually shape the community's image of the church. Our intention is to encourage people to try one of our weekend worship services, which are structured with unchurched visitors in mind. They are not seeker-centred, but they are seeker-sensitive. We preach on issues that we believe are relevant to both Christians and non-Christians.

Every few weeks we invite those who have made the first step in their journey towards the church to come to a Newcomers Event. This is a non-threatening occasion in a relaxed atmosphere over tea and coffee, where we have the opportunity to get to know people better, and they can get to know us. We then invite them to a Newcomers Small Group, which meets in a home. People are often curious to see inside a vicar's home! The group meets for just eight weeks and ends with a meal. In this informal setting we explain what our church is all about, why we do the things we do, who the leaders are, what a Christian is, what communion and baptism are all about, and any other subject they want to discuss.

It is important to do all this in a non-patronizing way. Allow new people to tell their story, to ask questions and to put their point of view. People attend because they want to know more about the church before they make a commitment to it. What does it believe? What is its ethos and purpose? What makes it tick? Why do we do the things we do? An attitude of 'this is what we believe – take it or leave it' will not win people over. A willingness to discuss and explain will be far more effective.

Our Newcomers Group has been a vehicle for all kinds of people to find their way into our church family. Running three times a year over a period of four years, it has resulted in nearly 200 people joining the church. Some people go on to seeker groups such as Alpha, to learn the basics of the Christian faith. A few start with Alpha and, after completing that course, come to the Newcomers Group to discover more about the local church. Once they have experienced a sense of belonging in a small group, it is easier to encourage people to take further steps. They may go on to be baptized or to join the church.

Our strategy of connecting with the community is built around a four-point plan: knowing Christ, growing in Christ, serving Christ and sharing Christ. Our church mission statement reads: 'To honour God by leading people to become fully devoted followers of Jesus Christ, to build them up in their faith, and to equip them for ministry in the church and mission in the world.' Everything we do is intentionally designed to communicate the good news of God in a way that changes people's lives. The whole church is part of the process of communicating the faith, and all our preaching and teaching is integrated into this purpose. From many years' experience as a Christian minister, I can honestly say, it works!

7

The Role of Worship

Imagine going to Florence, Italy, where Leonardo da Vinci's painting of *The Last Supper* hangs on the wall of a monastery dining room. As you look at the painting, a guide quietly points out detail after detail of the painting, things you might have overlooked if, like me, you have limited artistic perception. It could turn out to be one of the most rewarding experiences with a piece of art that you have known. Later, as you try to analyse the experience, you may come to the conclusion that a lot of it had to do with the skilled guide. Yet your experience was with the painting, not with the guide. In fact, you may not even remember what he or she looked like. All you know is that whoever it was enabled you to have a relationship with a masterpiece of art. The guide was your enabler, your means towards a fuller understanding and appreciation of this magnificent painting. The guide was not the object of your attention, but the catalyst of an experience in which something powerful and memorable was communicated to you.

The role of the guide is similar to the role of all leaders of public Christian worship. If we concentrate on the leaders alone, then we shall fail to achieve an experience of worship in which God communicates with us and we with him.

I believe there is a difference between seeker-centred and seeker-sensitive worship. Seeker-centred worship makes the assumption that non-believers cannot worship. Most of what happens in the service is therefore non-participatory and led from the front. In seeker-sensitive worship, however, worship is shared in a way that is simply alive to the needs of those who are unfamiliar with church. Worship can, and should, take place, and if non-believers cannot yet worship in spirit and truth, they can at least witness worship and experience it for themselves in that way.

Worship and evangelism are closely connected. As Eddie Gibbs and Ian Coffey make clear,

> It is the worshippers' intimacy with God and the genuineness and intensity of their devotion that make a powerful impact on seekers, preparing their hearts to receive the message that follows.[1]

When the prophet Isaiah went into the temple at a time of national crisis (Isaiah 6), he worshipped God in a way that resulted in the communication of forgiveness, clarity and purpose. In the active process of worship, by means of outward symbols, he heard God speaking to him, and he spoke to God: 'Here am I. Send me!' (v. 8). It was a time of powerful communication, and all in the context of worship.

Sadly, for many people, 'church' means 'dull, boring and irrelevant'. Worship services have become the biggest barrier to the unchurched. This includes the whole worship experience, the physical environment, the music, and the sermon. Boring, predictable and lifeless worship, and sermons which are irrelevant to everyday concerns, are some of the reasons why many have either left the church or show little or no interest in attending. Again, as Gibbs and Coffey point out,

---

[1] Eddie Gibbs and Ian Coffey, *Church Next*, IVP, 2001, p. 176.

Lifeless, meaningless worship will inevitably put off the new-comer who is not yet a believer. But in the heartful worship of a people surrendered to him, God is pleased to dwell in the praises of his people. Unbelievers are also likely to sense the presence of God.[2]

Let us make sure we are not creating barriers for seekers. If the way believers get together with God makes it hard for seekers to get together with God, then there is something wrong with the way we meet. At one of our worship services – and we do try to be seeker-sensitive – someone asked after we had said the 'Grace' to each other, 'What were you all looking at? Who were you looking for?' At least let us have the courtesy to put the words on a screen or in a leaflet, so that the seekers can take part as well. Seeker-sensitive worship does not mean eliminating the use of the Lord's Prayer; it means making the words accessible so that every-one can join in.

Worship is involvement

Archbishop William Temple's definition of worship is still one of the finest I have read.

The submission of all our nature to God; the quickening of the conscience by his holiness; the nourishment of the mind with his truth; the purifying of the imagination by his beauty; the opening of the heart to his love; the surrender of the will to his purpose.[3]

If this is what happened to the Old Testament prophet Isaiah, then the pattern that is described in Isaiah 6:1–8 is a pattern of worship worth following. Whatever your style

---

[2] Ibid.
[3] William Temple, *Preaching in St John's Gospel*, Macmillian, 1939, p. 68.

of worship – traditional, contemporary, blended, seeker-sensitive, seeker-centred – what happened to Isaiah was communication with God, and that should be the purpose of all our worship.

Isaiah had an overwhelming sense of the presence of God. Every worship service needs to start with a clear reminder that we are in God's presence. The call to worship and the first songs can bring God's presence to mind. Having become aware of who God was, Isaiah then became aware of himself as 'a man of unclean lips'. Praise and adoration is followed by confession. The confession is from the heart and is followed by the assurance of God's cleansing and forgiveness: 'Your guilt is taken away and your sin atoned for.' Next comes the word: 'Then I heard the voice of the Lord saying, "Whom shall I send? And who will go for us?"' Finally comes the response of obedience: 'Here am I. Send me.' It would be great if every member of the congregation was so inspired to action!

How you include these different elements in your worship will be up to each individual church. However you do it, whatever style you choose, I would strongly recommend that each worship service should start with a clear reminder of who God is. This can be done with a song or hymn of praise that is well known and describes the attributes of God. It is a mistake to start a worship time, particularly when many visitors and unchurched people are present, with an unknown song, or one that is difficult for a crowd to sing. It is not the moment to teach something new. Save that until later. Please do not start the worship with a string of in-house notices either. Nothing puts off a visitor more quickly.

Starting in the right way is vital. Too many church services begin like a damp squib. The leader ambles into the service; sometimes their voice is not clear, either because he or she has misjudged the strength of their voice, or the sound system has not been tested before the service. A song, a hymn, or a group of songs can literally wake people up, physically, mentally and spiritually, to who God is. A good song gets people going; they cannot sing without using physical energy. And waking up the body will soon wake up the mind!

Like Isaiah, we then need to be honest with God. We are a vulnerable and needy people. Talk to God in prayers of confession. Build in times of silence and reflection. Do keep it moving, though. Prepare people taking part to be where they are supposed to be, ready to do their bit without delay. For example, waiting after a prayer or song for someone to make a long walk from the back of the church to read the Bible at the front is wasted time. Another practical point that I learned years ago is that, if the congregation is expected to stand for a song or hymn, get them accustomed to standing immediately the music begins. If, as in many churches (and this is an old habit that is dying hard), the congregation does not stand until the music introduction is over, they miss the first few words of the song. Not only does the singing get off to a shaky start, but people are not attentive to what they are singing in those first few words.

The assurance of God's love for us also needs to come through, in prayers, music, images on a screen, or through the preaching. As Isaiah did, we need to be reminded of God's unfailing readiness to forgive, to accept us, and to change us.

I believe the spoken message needs to be prepared for. Again, as with Isaiah, there is often so much rubbish in our hearts and minds that must be cleared away before we are ready and able to hear God speak. When we come into church, most of us are preoccupied with all sorts of things – and they are not necessarily bad things. We are just preoccupied. Although at first they may not recognize what is happening to them, unchurched people also value a good experience of worship, even if they are just watching and listening, because it helps to create an environment that is conducive to hearing the message. If worship is genuine and from the heart, then it makes 'a powerful impact on seekers, preparing their hearts to receive the message that follows'.

Finally, plan a time of response. Back up the message with various kinds of help, as suggested earlier in Chapter 5.

It is also essential to give careful attention to the links between the various items of a worship service. There can be a lot of 'dead time' between different elements. Work on minimizing those transitional times – as soon as one element ends, another should begin. This is important in gaining the confidence of the unchurched, and also focuses believers on what they are there for. Untidy, unprepared worship does not glorify God. Prayerfully and carefully prepared worship enables the Holy Spirit to work through the leaders, who should also have prepared for the service, and it does not rule out spontaneity.

I have become aware through my involvement in televised worship of just how much time can be wasted. At Frinton there have been a number of occasions when we have broadcast our worship services live on national television and radio. On all of these occasions we have surprised ourselves at how many elements of worship can be included in under an hour. On Easter Sunday 1997, for example, we broadcast our second service on the UK ITV network. The worship included eight hymns and songs, the baptism by immersion of four people, each of whom told their story and were prayed for individually, a children's message, a children's song, a sung duet, three prayer times, a twelve-minute sermon and a closing prayer. All within 55 minutes and 40 seconds! That is not to say that worship services should always be less than one hour long, but it does illustrate how much time is usually wasted. More interestingly, and perhaps more significantly, the response of both the congregation in church and the viewers and listeners at home has been that the worship did not seem hurried. The many letters and telephone calls we have received following our occasions on air have taught us that commitment to excellence is a commitment that God can use powerfully.

If the church is to be healthy, it must offer a quality of worship that fortifies the values of the believer and at the same time attracts, appeals and relates to the unchurched. From the first days of the Christian church, both unbelievers and believers have been present in worship (1 Corinthians 14:23).

Rick Warren says, 'Making a service comfortable for the unchurched doesn't mean changing your theology. It means changing the environment.'[4] The biblical principle is clear. Although worship is an activity of believers, it can be a positive and relevant witness to unbelievers. How can we best achieve this?

It will not necessarily be by changing the style of worship. The experience of many churches is that the quality, not the style, of worship makes it a positive experience for both believer and unbeliever. Whether the style is traditional, contemporary or charismatic, a commitment to excellence changes worship from a negative to a positive experience. If the worship service is to be a witness, let it express confidence, energy, enthusiasm and expectancy. Believers may be tolerant of poor-quality worship, but unbelievers often expect more.

Worship is happening

In the twenty-first century, people are used to seeing, feeling and participating, rather than being spectators. If an older person missed church, they might ask of someone who was there, 'What was said?' A much younger person in the same

---

[4] Rick Warren, *The Purpose-Driven Church*, Zondervan, 1995, p. 244.

situation is more likely to ask, 'What happened?' Worship in the Bible is nearly always shown as a happening, a participation in events with all the senses. The language of God is the language of events – actions, occurrences, happenings. Jesus is the embodiment of the God who acts. The Lord's Supper, or communion, involves taste, smell, action and touch, as well as seeing, hearing and thinking.

An interesting development today is the mixing of ancient tradition and modern technology. Some churches mix sixth-century liturgy with alternative rock, and monastic visual images with high technology. In some places, this mix is attracting a whole new generation of people to church, often referred to as 'Gen-X'. As one clergyman said, 'Our musicians can rock out, but at the same time we use a lot of the traditional hymns.' Some church leaders believe that the twenty-first-century church will include a mix of styles – elements of Celtic Christianity, contemplative worship, traditional and contemporary – all combined with today's technology, using film clips, other visual images, variations in lighting, alternative rock and traditional hymn singing. These styles are likely to come alongside each other, rather than one style replacing another. Churches that have traditional styles of worship will not necessarily ignore the trends of postmodern worship.

Whatever the style of worship, ancient or modern, we always need to rediscover God the Holy Spirit in new, vital ways. The English word 'enthusiasm' literally means 'in God', or 'God within us'. If we only knew him better, many of the inhibitions that keep us from expressing our true feelings would fall away, and we could experience a joy and freedom that we have not always known in church.

One of the eight quality characteristics for a healthy church mentioned by Christian Schwarz in his book *Natural Church Development* is 'inspiring worship'.

While the question whether a church service targets primarily non-Christians has no apparent relationship to church growth, there is indeed a strong correlation between an 'inspired worship experience' and a church's quality and quantity.

Schwarz defines 'inspiring' as follows. It is

to be understood in the literal sense of inspiratio and means an inspiredness which comes from the Spirit of God. Whenever the Holy Spirit is truly at work (and His presence is not merely presumed), He will have a concrete effect upon the way a worship service is conducted including the atmosphere of a gathering. People attending truly 'inspired' services typically indicate that 'going to church is fun'.[5]

This kind of worship, whether it is in a traditional or contemporary setting, communicates. It communicates in a way that enables people to connect with God and to connect with each other. It can also connect with the community. Seekers can witness Christian worship and be attracted by its warmth, its vitality and its relevance.There is nothing so discouraging as worship services that seem to be going nowhere, that are just routine occasions. When that happens people go to 'a service' and there is no sense of forward movement. Nothing is happening. Worship is simply perfunctory. This kind of atmosphere does not attract crowds.

We should all be trying to build a spiritual momentum that helps people understand in every worship service that the church is on a journey with God and with people. We are seeking to grow as individuals and as a congregation in our relationship with God, with one another, with the community and with the world. Such a sense of expectation, journey and purpose is quickly detected by the visitor. In every

---

[5] Christian Schwarz, *Natural Church Development*, Church Smart Resources, 1996, p. 31.

church I have had the privilege of leading, this sense of journey and anticipation of the future has been a vital principle. I believe it is biblical. Paul writes to the Colossians:

> All over the world this gospel is bearing fruit and growing, just as it has been doing among you since the day you heard it and understood God's grace in all its truth. (Colossians 1:6)

Let this sense of purpose breathe through the whole church.

PART 4

The Word for Today

8

How to Use the Media

A religious affairs correspondent for a well-known national newspaper said at a press conference for church leaders, 'The church has a responsibility to communicate the gospel, and the media is one way of doing that.' A senior executive producer of an ITV company said, 'The church has the best news in the world. Why don't they use the media to communicate it?' 'Because we're not allowed to,' is the answer that is sometimes given, but that answer is not totally true. When ITV began a new series of televised programmes on a Sunday morning, for example, they sent the following note to all church leaders and church communication directors:

> ITV's flagship religious magazine programme is planning a tour of Britain – and we need your help.
>
> Each week, the team will be focusing on the faith of a different city, town or village with a potent mix of music, praise and testimony. We're looking for extraordinary stories of lives touched by God, powerful evangelism and faith in action.
>
> We want to give some of the country's best preachers a chance to spread the word on network television – and some of the best choirs, singers and musicians the opportunity to lead worship in hundreds of thousands of homes across Britain.

Maybe you know someone whose faith is driving them in extraordinary ways, someone who is making a real difference to their community, someone whose life has been transformed by their beliefs.

Maybe you know a pastor or priest with real charisma who has touched the lives of many – or a truly talented choir or worship group that deserves national recognition.

If so – please contact us now.

The response to this awesome opportunity could be counted on the fingers of two hands. It is a myth to believe that the Christian gospel cannot be communicated by television in the UK. It can, and I have heard and seen it done many times. The point of difficulty is not the gospel, but how it is presented. If it is presented positively, creatively and in a relevant way, it can be astonishingly effective.

The evidence for this can be seen in such programmes as *Bethlehem Year Zero*, which told the story of the events surrounding the birth of Christ as though they happened in the year 2000. More than 17 million people watched the ITV series over six days during Christmas 1999. On the 22nd December, 4.3 million viewers watched the programme, representing 27 per cent of all viewers that night. Again, on Christmas Day the number of viewers reached 4.8 million, representing 26 per cent of viewers across the channels. The viewing figures were the best for religious programmes on ITV since 1990. During Easter 2000, *Dateline Jerusalem* (telling the story of the events surrounding the arrest, crucifixion and resurrection of Christ as though they happened today) drew a viewing audience across the series on ITV of 12.8 million. These programmes were co-produced with CTVC. Another three-part television series broadcast in 2001, *Son of God*, reached millions of viewers on the first night. In the late summer and autumn of the same year, the broadcaster David Frost presented a series of ten programmes called *Alpha –*

Will It Change Their Lives? It followed participants on an Alpha course as taught by Nicky Gumbel.

It is not only committed Christians who are involved in making programmes about Christ, however. The study of Jesus has become a fiercely competitive industry in which believers and unbelievers, agnostics, Christians and Jews all fight for resources and exposure. It is true that in these cases no direct appeal to the viewer to become a Christian – or a Muslim, for that matter – can be made, but the facts can be presented. In a broadcast Christian worship service, of course, the preacher can make an appeal to the congregation with the cameras watching.

The Independent Television Commission Programme Code for religious programmes on ITV makes the boundaries clear about what can, or cannot be done.

> 7.6 Religious programmes may quite properly be used to propound, propagate and proclaim religious belief but neither programmes nor follow-up material may be used to denigrate the beliefs of other people. Religious programmes on non-specialist channels may not be designed for the purpose of recruiting viewers to any particular religious faith or denomination.
>
> A programme designed for the purpose of recruiting viewers is one which includes a message or challenge directed specifically at viewers rather than, for example, at a congregation or other group appearing in the programme. A 'specialist' service is a religious channel licensed under Schedule 2 Part II paragraph 2 of the Broadcasting Act 1990.
>
> 7.7 It is quite proper for a religious body or member of it positively to advocate the merits of a particular religious belief, or view of life but religious programmes must not persuade or influence viewers by preying on their fears.

No television or radio station wants a boring, dull and irrelevant programme. The same five principles thus apply in broadcasting as in preaching:

1. An excellent knowledge of the Bible.
2. A good command of language.
3. A compassionate heart for people.
4. An ability to relate theology to everyday life.
5. A passionate enthusiasm when preaching.

Christian communicators cannot ignore the 'how to say it' factor. As with preaching, delivery and presentation are vital and can make the difference between an acceptable programme and a very good programme. Christian radio and television programmes must command an audience. In the past a great deal of Christian programming has either been mandated or has been seen as part of the public broadcasting remit, and therefore the church in the UK has taken it for granted. We have had access to broadcasting for free. We think we have a right to it, while in many other countries, the church has had to pay. Today in the UK, however, programmes containing Christian values must compete for audiences in the same way as other programmes.

Apart from a need for Christians to be prepared to make and fund creative, relevant, watchable and theologically responsible programmes, there are a variety of other opportunities commonly presented to Christians in the UK to connect with the media. This is a vital resource and an unmissable opportunity to share the gospel. It is essential that we understand how to deal with the media and how to convey our message in the most effective way.

Practical pointers

Understanding the media

Take time to discover how the world of broadcasting works. Try to understand the pressures on the radio or television stations, on the producers, directors, researchers, etc. Many people criticize the media without understanding the limitations of the technology, the disciplines involved in programme-making, the pressure of keeping to a budget, the time constraints and the primary objective of attracting viewers or listeners. Try to get an idea of what works on television and radio, and what does not work.

Connecting locally

The simplest way to 'connect' locally is to use your local newspapers and radio stations. Many local radio stations have a free 'What's On' information service. Almost all local newspapers have a community affairs section.

Give radio stations about a week's notice and newspapers two or three weeks' notice for whatever event you wish to publicize. Try to get to know the names of your local researchers and journalists, and build their confidence in you. If you do a good job, they may well come back to you for news of future events or for comment on wider concerns. A journalist from one local newspaper now makes a regular personal visit to our church offices.

Learning how to write a good press release is invaluable. Journalists are busy people and do not have time to read through long epistles. If they realize that you understand something about how their world works, that will help to build the relationship. Tell them as simply as possible what you are doing, where you are doing it, when, and who for. Always leave a contact name, telephone number or e-mail address for further information.

The facts are not the only important feature in a good press release, however. It is also vital to think about how you can 'sell' the story. You want your story to come to the top of the pile of a busy news editor's desk, so make sure that the title will grab the attention of whoever reads it. For example, 'Last Drink of Clean Water for Two Weeks' could be an effective headline for a news item about a team of youngsters going to a remote part of the world for a short-term mission trip. Such a headline is more likely to catch the eye than, say, 'Church Youth Group Travel to South America'.

Connecting regionally and nationally

If you are writing a press release for a television station rather than the local paper, then the approach will need to be rather different.

First, it will be necessary to think in very visual terms. In fact, it is really not worth sending a press release to a television station unless what is happening has a highly visual dimension.

Second, you will need to try to give your story an extra edge and a wider relevance, in order to attract the larger audience available to you. The story will have more impact if you can link what you have to say with something of a more general or national interest. For example, when the World Cup was taking place, our church chose to show the games on our big screen. This was of interest to the press because it was happening at church instead of the usual pub venue – and then we had a high-profile referee come to talk about his faith a few Sundays later.

Michael Talbot told me, 'If you are trying to get air time, think laterally. A "story" about a church organising Christmas lunches for the homeless isn't going to make it (no crews on Christmas Day for a start). But find someone with a fantastic personal story to tell who came last year and ended up joining the church – then the local TV station might give the project some pre-publicity. Above all, it's personal testimony that works every time – strong, well-told stories of how faith has changed people's lives.'

All the points made above are matters for us to bear in mind when we are approaching the media. It may happen, of course, that a radio or television station might approach the church or church leader for news or a point of view on some topical issue. You might even be asked to participate in one of a number of different types of programmes. Once again, there are some practical points to consider – outlined below – and if you have thought about them beforehand, so much the better. Anything you can do which will help you to communicate your message more effectively is worth some careful thought.

Interview tactics

When clergy and other Christian leaders are invited to be interviewed by radio or television, many regard it as an ordeal instead of an opportunity. It does not have to be this way. Such invitations are precious chances to promote Christian values and principles, to correct misinformation, to give your own point of view, to launch an initiative or to campaign for your particular cause. If you are properly prepared, the experience need not be an ordeal at all.

Good media training is readily available and well worthwhile. CTVC at Bushey, Hertfordshire, run training courses which can be individually designed for church and religious groups. CTVC used to be called the Churches' Television Centre and was established in the late 1950s by J. Arthur Rank. It has grown into a fine training facility as well as an independent television programme maker. I have discovered that the kind of help given in such courses may be obvious to some people, but it is totally new to most. Here are some of the points you are likely to be taught at CTVC.

Before the interview

Be ready to take control of the situation, even before you agree to do the interview. See it as a potential opportunity to put your point of view, and prepare thoroughly in advance. You are not necessarily under obligation to answer all the questions put by the interviewer.

Have three concise, well-focused points that you want to make, and plan to get the most important point across right at the beginning of the interview. State your conclusion first – then back it up. Whatever happens after that, you have made your main point. So often time runs out before the interviewee realizes it, and then you feel frustrated that your point was never made.

Know your weakest arguments, and before the interview be brutally honest with yourself and with your interviewer about what you know and what you do not know. Be aware of your strongest points too, and make sure they come across with evidence to support your argument. Use examples and stories that involve the listener or viewer. You might also want to think up a memorable phrase which summarizes your arguments and will stick in the minds of the listeners or viewers. As in sermons, being simple does not mean being simplistic or shallow.

During the interview

Be yourself. Use simple, conversational language, avoiding jargon.

Show that you care. Be prepared to show your passion, enthusiasm and commitment, and sometimes even anger. Television and radio tend to flatten rather than magnify personalities and expressions, so heighten your energy level to compensate.

Listen carefully to all that is said. If the presenter gives wrong information or uses an unfair value judgement, challenge and correct it immediately, otherwise it will appear that you agree. If you cannot comment, explain why. Feel free to shift the focus. You can choose to highlight a particular example. Remember that you and the presenter are both after the same thing: an interesting interview which will engage the viewers or listeners.

Do not feel constrained by the question. Each question

can be a starting point or springboard for you to move to your own agenda. It is better, of course, not to highlight the fact that you are changing the subject or avoiding the question. Say, for example, 'The real issue here is this . . .' rather than, 'The real question you should ask is this . . .'

Do not waste time, and do not argue over irrelevant details. Avoid giving answers just to please the presenter. Be polite and friendly, but remember that you are the expert.

If the presenter appears confrontational, try not to over-react. That may be just what he or she wants you to do. If you lose your temper, you will lose the viewers' sympathy.

Do not allow words to be put into your mouth. If the presenter tries to summarize what you are saying, it is usually a clue that you are not being sufficiently clear or concise.

Remember the media needs good interviewees. The better you are, the more likely it is that you will be asked back.

Television

In a television interview, your appearance is an added dimension to consider. It is widely accepted that the single most important factor in communicating on screen is the way you look. Your face, dress, hair, body language, general appearance and demeanour all matter. Like it or not, that is the reality. Some of this is simply practical: clothes which have dots, small checks or stripes, or vast areas of black or white, for example, do not work well with the cameras. What you look like, and where you are if it is an outdoor interview, will say more about you than any words you speak. Appealing on behalf of the poor while leaning on your Rolls-Royce or BMW simply will not work!

Glasses and heavy fringes can also be a problem, as they can shadow your eyes. Thin frames are better than thick ones, plain glass is better than tinted, and photo-sensitive lenses should be avoided altogether.

Good eye contact with the interviewer is essential, unless

you want to look shifty! Do not lean away from the interviewer, as that will make you look nervous and defensive. Sit
alert and upright, or lean slightly forward. Take every
opportunity to smile. At the end of the interview, stay still
and attentive.

Radio

Even though your audience cannot see you on radio, use
your hands as you talk, to give life to your voice. Use
ordinary, chatty language, and avoid literary phrases.
Remember, a smile or a frown will affect how you say something, and it is vital to add interest and expression to your
voice.

Look at the presenter: although eye contact is not as
important as on television, you will be able to read interest
and boredom, or misunderstanding, on his or her face.
Looking at the interviewer also helps to make the conversa-
tion feel more normal. The radio microphone is not a public
address system.

Give plenty of examples and illustrations, because people
are always interested in stories. Unexplained jargon, abbreviations or initials are best avoided, because they simply
exclude the listeners. It is best not to take reams of notes to
a radio interview, as the paper will rustle and the microphone picks up every sound. For the same reason, avoid
fiddling with your pen or tapping the table!

Other types of programme

As well as giving interviews, church leaders and clergy are
sometimes invited to take part in group discussions on television or radio. Usually in this kind of programme, several
points of view are represented. Nobody seriously expects an
issue to be resolved there and then. The purpose of the programme is to give the listeners or viewers different viewpoints

or arguments on the same subject. In a group discussion, the amount of time you get to speak will largely depend on you.

Get yourself involved. Look at whoever is speaking, or whoever you are speaking to. If you are on television, avoid looking at the cameras. And do not hold back – the most committed participant often appears to have won the argument. Never lack conviction, but always be prepared to listen to what others have to say. A professional attitude, an air of authority and a sense of humour will all come over well. Even when you are not speaking, a dismissive laugh or a shake of the head will be picked up by the cameras and can be a means of communicating your point without words.

Another type of television programme is the 'down-the-line' interview. This approach is often used when a television company wants to interview someone many miles away, or get an instant reaction to a story which has just broken. The interviewee and the presenter never meet. You may be invited to go to the nearest local television studio or to talk outside to a camera which is set up close to where you are. You will not be able to see the presenter. His or her voice will come to you through an earpiece, and you will be asked to look at the camera lens.

Many people find this uncomfortable, because talking to a camera lens is unnatural. Practise beforehand by talking to an inanimate object such as a teapot or goldfish bowl! (Never mind what the neighbours say.) If you look away from the lens during the interview, you will appear shifty or unconfident. Since you cannot see the face of the presenter, you will not be able to tell if the presenter understands you or not, so take greater care than ever about how you express your point. Heighten the warmth and passion in your voice to overcome the strangeness of the technology. Although a 'down-the-line' interview may feel uncomfortable, it can be a powerful and effective way to communicate. You may be looking straight at the viewer as you deliver your message, so maintaining eye contact with the lens and speaking with conviction will give what you have to say even greater strength.

The radio equivalent of this is a telephone interview. The radio station may phone you and ask you to take part in a live interview in five or ten minutes' time, or you may get more notice if it is to be recorded for later use. Make sure you understand the nature of the interview and ask some basic questions before agreeing to take part. You might ask, for example, 'Who else is taking part?', 'Will it be live or recorded?', 'If recorded, will it be edited?', 'What kind of programme will it be used in?', 'Why are you asking me to be interviewed?' When you have found out all you can about the interview, give yourself time to consider whether you want to do it, then call back with your answer. If it is a recorded programme that is not going to be broadcast for several days, or even weeks, try to watch or listen to the programme to get an idea of its style.

Once you have agreed to appear or participate in any broadcast programme, the hard work of preparation really begins. Most programmes impose a discipline on us that preaching a Sunday sermon rarely does. We might be better communicators if it did!

Surfing the Net

Modern communications technology presents a particular challenge to the church. It means that the church can communicate well beyond its own four walls. Many churches across the world have invested in radio and television, and more recently the Internet. Needless to say, this is a mixed blessing. We are all aware of the excesses of the American-style televangelists. Nonetheless, just because something is sometimes done badly it does not mean that it should not be done at all. There are some good examples of churches using modern technology to reach out into their communities and beyond.

Some churches put their worship services on the Internet for the benefit of church members who cannot be physically present in the church. Some Christian organizations use the Internet to share their story and hopefully communicate it to an audience beyond their own faithful members.

The Internet, like most things, has a double potential. If there is an argument for a Christian presence in radio and television, there is an even stronger argument for a responsible Christian presence on the Net. It connects people with common interests all over the world. This has a massive potential for good. It also connects people with extremely unhealthy interests. A whole collection of sites exhibit bizarre spiritual behaviour and deviation from the true message of the Christian gospel. There are also websites which go way beyond pornographic interest, sites of which the vast majority of people are unaware. These sites graphically display or describe extreme acts of violence, mostly against women. There used to be (and perhaps there still is) an advert for the Web's 'sickest sites'. How much of an influence the dark side of the Internet has on people is hard to measure. Even though it may never be cleaned up, however, let us use the Net for communicating in a creative way the Christian values and content of the gospel.

There are some excellent Christian sites on the Internet. There are good preachers, good churches and organizations showing what people are able to do for the poor and deprived communities of the world. This wealth of good Christian content informs, educates and influences for good many Internet surfers. Christians can now become missionaries in nearly every country of the world, without leaving their own home. How can that happen? We shall see in the next chapter.

9

Communicating Across the World

A few months ago, a friend of mine in California e-mailed me to say he had noticed on our church website that we were sending a team of young people on a short mission trip to Brazil. He had just returned from Fortaleza, the same city to which our young people were going. He had spent some time with the minister of a church there, and he wanted to help link that minister with our church and youth team. Through the Internet, a link was made that otherwise would not have been made, and our youth team were able to worship in a church they would otherwise have missed.

The Internet is providing a host of new opportunities. It is a new medium for communicating the gospel. 'Christians have an unprecedented opportunity online to reclaim lost people,' says Thomas Wright, Internet evangelism co-ordinator for the North American Mission Board.

We are told that there are over 310 million people online globally. Part of the overall evangelism strategy of churches might be to train some of their people to respond to those online who raise spiritual questions. Taking part in message forums is a way of engaging people with the gospel. After the collapse of the World Trade Center on the 11th September

2001, there were message forums that were full of faith-based questions and discussion.

Many people are now using the Internet to find answers to their spiritual questions, and this is a rapidly developing area of ministry. It is estimated that by 2010 as many as 50 million individuals may be relying solely on the Internet to meet their spiritual needs. There is already a mass of archived religious material available. Many people read online devotionals, and buy religious products and resources through the Net. Of course, some of the 'resources' are less than helpful – some of the self-produced and self-marketed services are definitely best avoided – but there are many good things too. Some churches, for example, use the Internet to allow their housebound members, or people away on business, to worship at the same time as everyone else in their church.

People of all ages are learning to use the Internet. In our own church, there are people in their seventies and eighties who have familiarized themselves with it, and that trend will continue. People of working age who have home PCs and have been connected to the Internet will probably stay connected after retirement. At the present time, however, it is young people who are among the most frequent users of the Internet. A study of 12- to 17-year-olds, released by the Pew Internet and American Life Project, said that about 73 per cent of US teenagers use the Internet and say it plays a significant role in their relationships with family and friends. 'They also habitually multi-task, performing several Internet activities simultaneously.' One teenager who responded to the survey said, 'I get bored if it's not all going at once because everything has gaps – waiting for someone to respond to an IM [instant message], waiting for a website to come up, etc.' The study shows that the Internet is changing the way teens interact with their friends. For instance, 37 per cent of those responding said they have used instant-messaging to write something they would not have said in person. It is the same as text-messaging on mobile phones. For more information on the survey, there is a full 46-page report available free online at: http://www. pewinternet.org/reports/pdfs/PIP_Teens_Report.pdf

Making best use of the Internet

The Internet is a great way for churches and church leaders to communicate with other churches and leaders around the world. It is an excellent tool for research and resources. Patrick Dixon, in his book *Cyberchurch*, published in 1997, writes,

> The Internet is quite simply the largest, most powerful and fastest library you could possibly find – as well as the fastest growing. Where else can you locate 50 million documents so easily?[1]

That was five years ago. If it is, as Dixon says, 'the fastest growing' library, how much bigger is it today? It is also a speedy method of sharing ideas. Clergy and lay people can share vast resources and experiences of church ministry and mission. Sermon preparation should be easier and quicker with the help of the Net!

The Internet is proving invaluable as a fast and effective way for churches to maintain communication with their own mission personnel in other countries. It is also an opportunity for individual Christians to engage in mission. The Internet provides opportunities to communicate the gospel where Christians themselves cannot go. We can now go 'into all the world' without leaving our own homes.

The Internet can provide many more people with an opportunity to share in your worship. Dr Paul Cho, Pastor of the Central Church in Seoul, South Korea, sees the

---

[1] Patrick Dixon, *Cyberchurch*, Kingsway, 1997, p. 85.

Internet as having enormous potential. On one occasion, when he was in Dubai, 3,000 people attended his evening meetings. When some of these people were asked how they knew about the meetings, they replied, 'Through the Internet. In Saudi Arabia we have no church – we can't own a Bible, but we can still use the Internet. We were watching your worship on the Internet and you announced you were coming to Dubai, so we have come.'

Local churches can combine the benefits of being online with using modern communications technology in worship. We shall look more closely at these opportunities in the next chapter.

Local churches can also set up their own website. Not only is this a communication tool to be used for the benefit of its own church members and congregation, but it also enables outsiders to discover more about the church in an anonymous and non-threatening way. Nonetheless, setting up and maintaining a website is a big commitment, and a number of questions should be asked before going ahead.

1. Who is the website for?

What will be the primary purpose of your website? Is it to provide your own members with information? Is it a way of helping your own people to share ideas, to know what is going on in the church, and to keep in touch with one another? If it is, that is OK, but remember that your site will have outside visitors and will therefore need to be visitor- or seeker-sensitive.

Perhaps you want the website to attract to the church people who live in the area or who have recently moved into the community and who want a church to go to. There are a number of good examples of this kind of church website. If this is the direction in which you want to move, it is well worthwhile spending some time doing research by looking at as many existing church websites as you can.

Do not assume that people who visit the site will be mostly those with some kind of church background. You may want your website to be more evangelistic. This kind of website will be designed not to keep your own members informed or to attract Christians moving into your area to come to your church, but to present the gospel directly to non-Christians. Such a site might attract people by using headlines and statements that address current issues. Remember, the Internet provides a non-threatening platform for seekers.

Another kind of website you might consider is similar to a 'welcome to the community' type of leaflet for those new to the neighbourhood. It should list the names and locations of local chemists, doctors' surgeries, hospitals, banks, schools, police station, etc. Such a website can be a point of contact for the whole community and the only mention of the church would be as the sponsor or maintainer of the site. One example of such a site is run by a church in Teddington, and it is called 'Wot? – What's Online for Teddington?' Colin Hicks, who maintains the site, says, 'The only connection with the church apparent to the casual visitor is that it is sponsored by the church – and so it has advertising banners for the church's activities like any other sponsored site on the Internet. It steps right over into the community by carrying information on all local societies, websites, etc. Even places to find real ale. We have a clearly stated editorial policy on the website, but we have deliberately adopted a non-exclusive stance.' Colin adds that this kind of website could be considered by a church as a second site.

2. Who is going to run the site?

Designing and maintaining a church website is a huge commitment. An out-of-date website is like an out-of-date noticeboard outside the church: very off-putting. It needs to be organized by someone with a vision for it – someone with enthusiasm, but also with experience and skill in the necessary technology, and a commitment for the future. Ideally, it can be managed by a team with an experienced team leader.

Running a website means applying some of the best practices involved in producing a church paper or magazine. The first page is all-important. It needs to reflect the answer to the question, 'Who is this for?' It needs to show clearly what is on offer – 'What's on the menu?' and 'What's new?' You want people to visit the site not just once, but many times. A good church website will be updated at least once a week.

3. Who will be your Internet Service Provider (ISP)?

Most ISPs offer website facilities to subscribers as part of their service. The church also needs to consider hardware and software. This can be expensive if the church is not already online. There are various hosts to research. Some offer free church webpages to churches which have no site of their own, and many companies offer reasonably priced webhosting and domain registration (especially for .org.uk and .co.uk domains). The best approach is to search the Internet for existing good church websites and ask them directly about their ISP and host facilities.

Guidelines for using the Net

Having chosen a provider, do not be over-ambitious in getting a website up and running. Start with one or two basic pages of information about your church, and build up the site as you gain experience and learn from others.

The Methodist Church in the UK has provided its churches with a very helpful list of guidelines which have been adopted by other churches and denominations as well.

With their permission, I reproduce it here with the recommendation that these guidelines are followed for your own protection and the protection of the individuals in your church and community.

Anyone designing a website for a church, circuit or district will want to ensure that it promotes opportunities for all ages – including children and young people – to get involved in the life of the church. While it is important to reflect the full mix of participation in church worship and other activities, care should be taken to ensure the safety of children and young people. Website builders are encouraged to follow these guidelines:

- Children and young people under the age of 18 should not be identified by surname or other personal details. These details include e-mail or postal addresses, telephone or fax numbers.
- When using photographs of children and young people, it is preferable to use group pictures. When a photograph of an individual child or young person is used, surnames or other personal details should not be used in any caption.
- Permission to use information about or photographs of children and young people – where they are to be identified – should be obtained from their parents or carers.
- Care must be taken when advertising special events for children and young people. It may be beneficial to encourage enquirers to obtain full details for an event by speaking to a responsible contact person, such as a youth worker or minister. (For example, a notice for a district event might give the type of event, the date, the age group, the town or circuit, but not the specific venue. A church holiday club for children might not give specific times, but might talk about 'two hours every morning'. In each case a telephone contact of an organizer/leader is included.)

When posting activity ideas for children's or youth groups, they should comply with good safeguarding practice. There may be occasions when church officers, youth or children's workers wish to demonstrate the Internet to children or young people, or encourage them to access information online as part of an activity. When this happens, workers are encouraged to follow these guidelines:

- Ensure that parents or carers are aware of what their children or young people are doing and have given their permission.
- When demonstrations are being given, plan beforehand to ensure that all websites visited have material that is appropriate for the age group taking part.
- Where children and young people are given access to undertake their own searches on the Internet, the following search engines are recommended by the Department for Education and Employment (DfEE):
  – AOL Net Find Kids only
  – KidsClick web search for kids by librarians
  – PowerBug
  – Superkid
  – Webkeys Prowler world's biggest search engine for kids
  – Yahooligans! Web guide for kids

Your nearest Local Education Authority may also operate a local search engine facility appropriate for children and young people.

- Where children and young people are being encouraged to undertake subsequent searches on the Internet back home, make sure that they do so with the knowledge/supervision of their parent or carer.
- Warn children and young people about the dangers of giving out personal details on the Net.
- Ensure children and young people obtain parental consent if they wish to develop Internet friends into face-to-face friendships. Even then, they should always be accompanied on any first meeting.

Further guidelines for children and young people can be found in the NCH Action for Children paper 'Children on the Net: Opportunities and Hazards' (1998).

The Internet is a tool. Like any other tool, once it is put into the hands of the Holy Spirit, it can be used effectively.

> The Church must always be alert to the moving of the Spirit. He leads continually into new spheres, ways and means of spreading the Gospel. Society changes, so must the Church's methods to reach society. To fail to do so is to miss God's purpose for Church namely, to communicate dynamically to its day.[2]

Nonetheless, just as the church was reluctant to recognize the potential of radio, television, film and video, one wonders if it will make the same mistake with the Internet. Like the media generally, the world of the Internet seems easier to ignore than get to grips with. As the church needed to release people into broadcasting, so we will need to release people to train, understand and use the Internet for communicating the faith. Fulfilling the Great Commission is more possible than ever before, if we will only seize the opportunity.

Shane Nixon of Baptist State Convention, North Carolina, gives some examples of what to do and what not to do:

- *Do something*. Churches that make no effort in the area of technological ministry will lose members; this we know. My dad has a sign in his office that states: 'If all you are doing is nothing, how do you know when you are finished?' For churches, doing nothing in this area might mean they are finished!
- *Don't over do it*. This is a common pitfall. David Winfrey notes that 'too many church leaders are enamored by the gee-whiz technology . . .' and end up with good stuff their people can't or won't use. Sally Morgenthaller, founder of

---

[2] *What the Bible Says*, edited by Lewis Drummond, Marshall, Morgan and Scott, 1974, p. 164.

Worship Evangelism Concepts, speaks of a church in Scotland that tried to minister to teens. They used audio/visual displays and computer graphics. But their audio/visual material was from the 1980s and the graphics were from publications designed for older adults. The kids started their own church two miles away.

- *Do your homework*. Have a strategy. Preachers and Sunday school teachers do not dare perform their roles without a plan, nor do church committees and teams. Technology should be just as thought-out and organized.

- *Don't try to do it all yourself*. Get help. There are probably lay people in the congregation who would love to help. Implementing technology is not something most pastors learned in seminary. Call on the resources available to you – church members and maybe even your denomination.

- *Be willing to change the medium*. Our God is an awesome God. He's used burning bushes and still small voices. Why should we think He can't use computers and overhead projectors? Many people thought Billy Graham was crazy when he talked about doing television evangelism. Thank goodness he had the vision to recognize its worth!

- *Don't change the message*. God is still God. Whether presented through a PowerPoint presentation or an Internet site, leaders and learners still focus on the need for a relationship with God. So before you venture to employ new technologies in your ministry, recognize that you are not alone. Others have been there and some have even done it.[3]

For more information, consult these helpful resources:

- Technology for Worship Ministries, www.tfwm.com – a great place to find resources for technology vendors, industry conferences and networking.

---

[3] *The Biblical Recorder*.

- Pew Trust Internet studies, www.pewinternet.org – a great place for statistics, research and analysis of current data relating to churches and technology. Specifically you will want to read the report 'Wired Churches, Wired Temples'.

10

Modern Technology in the Local Congregation

How can modern technology help churches to be more effective in communicating their message? For the first five years of my ministry I preached with the naked voice. The building could seat about 200 people, but no one ever thought of installing a public address system. Today, even the smallest church building seems to have a sound system. In my second church I was excited that in front of the lectern was a microphone! Although I am grateful for the early discipline and training of using my voice without the help of a sound system, I revelled in the new opportunity for greater flexibility. The style of preaching and leading worship changes with a good sound system – you can be more conversational and still be heard clearly.

For years, many churches have used the humble tape recorder to provide housebound members with audio tapes of worship and other events. However, churches are notoriously slow in seeing the advantages of new communications technology, be that radio, television, newspapers or the Internet. Some churches chose some time ago to use overhead projectors to show hymns and songs on large screens, thereby dispensing with hymnbooks. Now a much greater technical revolution is taking place: PowerPoint displays and video projection.

Inevitably, in some churches there will be resistance to change. It seems as though the church is often reluctant to see the advantages of new technology, only focusing on the disadvantages or dangers. Hannah Whitall Smith, author of *The Christian's Secret of a Happy Life*, whose life spanned most of the nineteenth century, recalls that when railroads were first built they were considered a wicked tempting of Providence. When she bought her first sewing machine, she kept it in the attic as a secret because her friends thought it was 'such an awful machine', 'the offspring of Hell'. And in her father's day, she said, suspenders (braces) to hold up men's trousers were believed to have been invented by Satan!

When the proposal was made to put street lights in a New England town, the local paper gave four objections. The first was a theological objection: artificial illumination would interfere with the divine plan for the world, which ordained that it should be dark during the night hours. The second was a medical objection: emanations from illuminating gas would be dangerous, and lighted streets would incline people to remain outdoors, thus tending to increase the number of colds. The third objection was moral: the fear of darkness would vanish, and drunkenness and depravity would increase. The final objection was 'popular': if the streets were illuminated every night, such constant illumination would tend to rob festive occasions of their charm!

Today, the objections to using video and PowerPoint (or similar programs) in church range from comments such as, 'It detracts from the divinely ordained practice of preaching,' to, 'People have nothing to hold in their hands while singing,' to, 'It makes church more like a cinema.' If the new technology is properly and correctly used, however, it enhances the preaching, improves the singing of the congregation and, in a visual culture, helps people to follow and remember the sermon more easily.

Technological do's and don'ts

Don't overuse it

Churches frequently make this mistake and end up serving the technology instead of using the technology to serve the mission of the church. Make sure it improves the effectiveness of the communication rather than diminishes it. Set boundaries to ensure that it enhances the worship experience and does not detract from it. Used creatively and carefully, with good technical and theological preparation, it can be a powerful tool of communication. It can make prayer more meaningful through the use of images, either for praise or petition. It can educate the congregation about what is going on in other parts of the world through the use of video clips. It can help to broaden the congregation's understanding of world mission.

Do invest in good quality equipment

If your church is serious about being a missionary congregation communicating to the world outside in the hope of inviting them in, then it is worth investing in high quality technology. There is nothing worse than a screen that does not show clearly either the words or the images.

If you buy a projector that has to be positioned within a few feet of the screen, then the projector, laptop computer and operator are in danger of cluttering the front of the church – the area that most people see while they worship. An untidy platform area detracts from worship. It can create a mixed message. We may say we care, and we are relevant, but a carelessly arranged platform area can so easily indicate the opposite.

Do be prepared to train those using it

It does not help communication if words and symbols come on the screen at the wrong time, or remain on the screen too long. It is also a distraction if they come up in the wrong order.

It is worth identifying people who have an interest in this technology and are willing to undergo some basic training in how to use it. Train your operators one at a time and gradually build up a technical team. They will need to know how to manage the computer-generated text and visuals, plus the video-operating equipment. They will also need to know how to interchange them during the same service. All of this has to be co-ordinated with the sound system, which may also use CDs and audio tapes as part of the same occasion.

Do be thorough in the preparation of your material

As with most things, careful preparation is the secret of good presentation. A worship service which has been hurriedly put together benefits no one. That is just as true today with an ill-prepared PowerPoint presentation as it was 50 years ago when hymns were chosen at the last minute and prayers were prepared without sufficient time for thought about their content. All this, of course, still goes on today, but add to the mix a load of poorly prepared material on a large screen, and it becomes carelessness written large. No one benefits. If unchurched visitors are present, remember that they are likely to be less forgiving of sloppiness than Christians who are regular members of the congregation.

With many unchurched visitors, we sometimes only have one opportunity to communicate with them. If we blow it, they may never come back again. On more than one occasion in our church, we have had unchurched individuals tell us that they decided to try the church once, just to see what was happening. One man told us that he had tried most things in life without finding purpose and meaning. Out of the blue he decided to come to church one Sunday, just to see if God had anything to say. He had only been to church a few times as a child 40 years earlier. He said he was only going to give it a try once. He thought it was not going to make any difference to him, and that it probably would not mean anything, but he would give it one try. When you know you have people like this in your congregation, you become aware of a big responsibility. Happily, this man was greatly surprised at the relevance of the message and he has been attending our church ever since. This has happened with many others too.

If we can improve the quality of our worship and the relevance and clarity of our communication, then let us use the very best tools to do so.

Don't use it to turn sermons into lectures

Some preachers, when using multimedia projection, drift into a presentational or lecture style of delivery. This is very likely to happen if the speaker is also the person who controls the computer and changes the slides. Preaching is a unique form of communication, and technology should only be used to add to it rather than detract from what is being said. If another person can operate the projector, the preacher can prepare a script or list of cues to give to the operator, and then should be able to forget the screen and preach as he or she normally would, with complete freedom of movement.

Do choose colours and backgrounds carefully

Some colours make it difficult for words and images to be seen, particularly in bright daylight. Some dyslexic people can also find reading the words very difficult if certain colours are used as a background or for the text itself. Use colours and backgrounds that are in sympathy with the message.

Do use good quality videos

People today are becoming used to high-quality pictures on their home television screens and in cinemas. Poor quality images in church do nothing for our worship or communication. Again, regular members of the congregation who are already believers will be far more forgiving of second-rate standards than those who come to church less often.

Steve Williams of Bold Assurance Ministries in the United States has compiled what he calls the *Seven Deadly Sins of Ineffective PowerPoint*.

Deadly sin No. 1

Too little contrast is the result of using text and backgrounds of similar colours. 'A basic rule is there should be enough contrast between them so text can be easily read. The greatest contrast is white text on a black background or black text on a white background.'

Deadly sin No. 2

Too many colours used for text and objects can result in a rainbow effect. 'The brain tries to figure out why are there so many colours, and if it's doing that, it's going offline.'

Two text colours per slide are usually enough to look good and be readable. Three different text colours are enough for an entire presentation.

'It is good to use different colours for the titles and body text, but try to use the same colour all the way through your presentation for titles and the same colour for body text. That will keep people's attention focused on you and not your presentation.'

Deadly sin No. 3

Too much text makes a slide look cluttered and hard to read. 'Use the five and 10 rule. Limit each slide to about five lines of text that can be read in about 10 seconds. Six lines are OK, seven if you have to . . . but when you get beyond that you have too much text.'

Williams says that if the presentation requires more text than his recommended maximum, it is best to automate the text so that it does not come on the screen all at the same time. Present part of it on half the slide, giving the viewer time to read it, then put the remainder up on the bottom half of the slide.

Deadly sin No. 4

Text that is too small means that people will have to strain to read it. 'This will distract them and cause them to miss hearing the point.'

'Step back and look at it yourself on a large screen,' Williams advises. 'If in doubt, make it larger.'

Deadly sin No. 5

Too many bullets make a presentation predictable and boring. 'Bullets are great if used sparingly and wisely, but I've seen presentations where the number of bullets used reached the regurgitating stage.'

Williams suggests using 'un-bullets' such as pictures, or placing text inside various shaped objects such as ovals, rectangles or circles.

Deadly sin No. 6

Too many transition effects can disorientate the viewer. 'Transition effects are used to change from one slide to another during a presentation. PowerPoint 2000 gives you 60 or 70 effects, but they shouldn't all be used in one presentation.'

Williams suggests using the K.I.S.S. principle with transition effects. 'That's "keep it simple, sweetheart". Use a maximum of two to three different effects throughout your whole presentation. Use them when you are switching content.'

Deadly sin No. 7

Using boring slides can put the audience to sleep. 'I've described a lot of excesses when creating slides, but underdoing it can be as bad as overdoing it,' Williams comments.

Effective use of colours and graphic objects can add appeal to presentations and make people want to watch them. Clip art, photos, WordArt and autoshapes help make slides more visually appealing when used correctly.

'By eliminating the seven deadly sins from your presentations, you will encourage your audience to focus on your message and learn more,' Williams says. 'And they won't think you started using PowerPoint yesterday.'

Managing change

New technology is wonderful when used well, but introducing it without due care and attention will only backfire. Prepare well, and use good quality material. Above all, avoid trying to do too much too soon. Take it step by step. There are a number of resource agencies which offer help for churches in this area. One is the Reaching the Unchurched network, which offers CD Roms containing PowerPoint presentations, a database of themes suitable for seeker services, videos and other multimedia resources. Their website is www.run.org.uk. The Saddleback Church in California provides a wide range of teaching and training resources to help ministers and pastors in their communication to both the churched and the unchurched. Their website is www.pastors.com.

Change will always bring some discontent. It was the same when the pipe organ was first introduced into congregational worship. In the 1970s and 80s many churches split over the use of other musical instruments besides the piano and the organ. Some of those same churches now have excellent music groups comprising a variety of instruments. Change is always controversial, however – particularly, it seems, in Christian churches. Some changes become unacceptable because they are not properly managed. Change always means learning new skills and grasping new ideas.

Inevitably, mistakes will be made, but with patience, a willingness to learn and a determination to aim for excellence in all things, your church will benefit from such changes. The guiding principle should be 1 Corinthians 10:31: 'Whatever you do, do it all for the glory of God.'

EPILOGUE

Communicating Your Vision

Where then do we begin the process of communicating the most needed message on earth – namely that Jesus said, 'I have come that they may have life, and have it to the full' (John 10:10)? Many of us are in churches that really need to change. If we do not change soon, those churches will quite likely decline and die. What are some of the basic steps we should follow now to get started?

The process must begin in the heart of the leader. Unless the leader of the church has a vision for change, it will never happen. Even if others in the church have a vision, it is in danger of being blocked, unless the leader can articulate and communicate it. Spend some time in prayer and Bible study, and listen to people in the community. Gather information about your community and its needs. Understand its culture and how best to communicate with that culture. Then learn how best to communicate the vision.

Jesus communicated his vision to his disciples, first by example and second by describing it. In John 13:14–15, after washing the disciples' feet, Jesus says, 'Now that I, your Lord and Teacher, have washed your feet, you also should wash one another's feet. I have set you an example that you should do as I have done for you.' Jesus left us an example. The apostle Paul said, 'Follow my example, as I follow the example of Christ' (1 Corinthians 11:1).

Church leaders also need to model their vision. Leaders would do well to spend less time in committees and more time in exercising ministry. In some churches, the elders, deacons, or even the PCC, are seen as policing bodies controlling what happens in the church. To communicate our vision we need rather to be seen *living out* that vision, as Jesus did, as well as spending time praying it through.

Symbolism is another powerful tool of communication. In years past, much more was made of images. Stained-glass windows, banners, ornaments and various other furnishings were all used to communicate what the church was about. Our church has a clock tower with four clock faces and this is a well-known landmark in the town. Using the symbol of the clock face, we encourage members of our congregation to 'Take Time for God' and learn how to know him better, to follow him, to serve him and to share him with others.

It is vital also to speak your vision. The spoken word has power. 'Take Time for God' is a simple statement that conveys instantly what we are inviting people to do. There is power in such statements. They are easily remembered. They can capture people's imagination. 'Growing Closer to God' is a statement we used one autumn and winter to keep before the congregation our intention to help them move forward on their journey of faith. On small cards, in the weekly bulletin, in sermons and on numerous occasions, we used this phrase as a reminder that we had set aside that particular season as a period when, as a church, we wanted to strengthen our faith and build a strong, close relationship with God.

Do not be afraid to repeat the vision. Halfway through rebuilding the walls of Jerusalem, after 26 days, the Old Testament leader Nehemiah repeated his vision. Jesus also repeated his vision. He said to the disciples at the beginning of his ministry, 'Come, be my disciples, and I will show you how to fish for people' (Mark 1:17 NLT). Then, at the end of his earthly ministry, he said, 'Therefore go and make disciples of all nations, baptising them in the name of the Father and of the Son and of the Holy Spirit, and teaching them to obey everything I have commanded you. And surely I am with you always, to the very end of the age' (Matthew 28:19–20). At least once more, just before his ascension, he said, 'But you will receive power when the Holy Spirit comes on you; and you will be my witnesses in Jerusalem, and in all Judea and Samaria, and to the ends of the earth' (Acts 1:8). What a great vision!

Spending time in personal contact with people is another essential element when it comes to communicating purpose and vision. Spend time with key people, as Jesus did when he spent time with the disciples. Spend time also with those who are struggling to understand the vision. Let them ask questions. Listening is part of communicating. Jesus listened to the people he met.

Communicate by making comparisons. Saying that something is 'as big as a double-decker bus' is a much more immediate and visual way of communicating size than just giving out dimensions. Jesus often said, 'The kingdom of heaven is like . . .' There is nothing wrong in suggesting that when a church is trying to find out about its local community, it is like engaging in a piece of market research. Help people to understand the purpose and vision of your church by making comparisons with familiar, everyday things.

Finally, communicate by meeting needs. James Emery White says,

I fear the contemporary church has become marked by a narcissistic attitude that places the individual needs and desires *of the believer* at the centre of attention. Much like the older brother in Jesus' story of the prodigal son, believers often act as if the fattened calf should be reserved for them and them alone.[1]

In Mark 10:51 Jesus asks Bartimaeus, 'What do you want me to do for you?' The blind man says, 'Rabbi, I want to see.' Jesus obliges. 'Go,' he says, 'your faith has healed you.' Immediately the blind man receives his sight and follows Jesus as he continues along the road.

Was Jesus responding to felt needs? Of course he was. Here is the grace of God in action. As I mentioned in Chapter 2, the broadcaster and producer Peter Brooks said nearly 20 years ago, 'We need to speak to their felt needs in such a way as to reach through them to deeper needs than ever they have been aware of.' This is precisely what Jesus was doing – by asking Bartimaeus what he wanted; by listening to his answer. Jesus met the man's obvious need, and in so doing also met a deeper need. The man 'followed Jesus'. I think he got the message!

That is precisely what we want people to do today: we want them to get the message. Let us not be too proud to learn from others in the non-religious as well as the religious world. Most of all, let us learn from the Master Communicator, Jesus Christ.

---

[1] James Emery White, *Rethinking the Church*, Baker, 1997, p. 126 (italics mine).

Shapes of the Church to Come

by Bishop Michael Nazir-Ali

As a leading Bishop in the Church of England, Michael Nazir-Ali could justly be called a pillar of the establishment. But this book is a clear demonstration that even the pillars realise that the building could collapse if radical changes are not implemented soon – changes that will involve a serious re-evaluation of the church's mission and ministry in today's world.

'This book provides thought-provoking insight on the most pressing issue facing the church today.'
Steve Chalke, Founding Director, Oasis Trust

'Bishop Michael Nazir-Ali explores some of the crucial questions facing churches in the next decade...'
John Reardon, OBE

'Rooted in Scripture and forged in pastoral practice, the key insights in this book address global and local issues that must not be ignored if the church is to stay alive and relevant.'
David Coffey, President, Baptist Union

FUTURE **CHURCH**

Liberated to Lead

by Colin Buckland

This unique book is designed to
enhance the effectiveness of full-
time leaders in Christian
ministry or mission. Used
prayerfully, the exercises and
points for reflection will enable
you to:

- balance family life and the
  pressures of ministry
- cultivate a healthy
  attitude to power in
  ministry roles
- settle on realistic
  expectations in ministry
- gain an introduction to self-awareness skills
- clarify your sense of calling to Christian service
- avoid unnecessary sexual problems
- overcome or prevent burnout

REVD COLIN BUCKLAND has more than 23 years'
experience as a pastor, and more than 18 years' as a consultant,
trainer and counsellor to church leaders, churches and
Christian organisations.

*FUTURE*CHURCH

Leadership Tool Kit

by Bryn Hughes

After nearly twenty years in management training, Bryn Hughes is convinced that enhancing the skills of leadership is critical for ministers of churches, leaders of missions and other Christian organisations. These skills come into sharp focus when training the crucial second tier of leadership.

However, leaders who are committed to improving both themselves and their senior teams are desperately short of practical tools. Here is a development manual of eleven tested tools, including:

- Exploring motives
- Identifying key result areas
- Learning from success – and failure
- Delegation and communication
- Continuing self-development

FUTURE**CHURCH**